Uncle Arthur's

BEDTIME
STORIES

Volume Three

Uncle Arthur's Bedtime STORIES

Volume Three/Arthur S. Maxwell

Published jointly by

PACIFIC PRESS®
PUBLISHING ASSOCIATION
Nampa, ID 83653
Oshawa, Ontario, Canada

REVIEW AND HERALD
PUBLISHING ASSOCIATION
Washington, D.C. 20039-0555
Hagerstown, MD 21740

Contents

1	Richard's Rubbish Heap	9
2	"I'm Here, Sir!"	14
3	A Boy in Chains	19
4	Tale of a Tangle	23
5	How Doris Lost Her Voice	29
6	Flaming Beacons	36
7	Peter and the Pumpkin Seed	41
8	Four Times as Much	49
9	One Naughty Lamb	54
10	The Story of Flight	58
11	Caught by the Tide	68
12	Little Shadow	77
13	Clouds at a Picnic	82
14	How Terence Got His Train	88
15	Steve the Steeplejack	94
16	The Mysterious Rider	101
17	The Forgotten Packages	110
18	Why Leslie Got Left	114
19	Daddy's Birthday Present	117
20	They Gave Their Best	122
21	Swami and the Crocodile	127
22	Digging for a Bicycle	133

5

◀ Painting By Russell Harlan

6

23 Alan and the Attic   138
24 Our World in Space   141
25 The People in Our World   148
26 God's Plan for Our World   152
27 Little Miss Grumbletone   158
28 Not on Purpose   163
29 On the TV   167
30 Present for Grandma   174
31 Frontiers of Peace   179
32 Jesus Knows and Cares   182
33 Honest Tommy   189

Lesson Index

ADVICE, TAKING
Tale of a Tangle 23

AIRPLANES
The Story of Flight 58

ANIMAL STORIES
One Naughty Lamb 54
Swami and the Crocodile 127

BIRD STORIES
Steve the Steeplejack 94

CARELESSNESS
Why Leslie Got Left 114

CHOOSING THE BEST
On the TV 167

CREATION
God's Plan for Our World 152
Our World in Space 141
People in Our World, The 148

DEPENDABILITY
Forgotten Packages, The 110
Peter and the Pumpkin Seed 41

DISOBEDIENCE
Alan and the Attic 138
How Doris Lost Her Voice 29
One Naughty Lamb 54

FAITH
Clouds at a Picnic 82

FAULTFINDING
Little Miss Grumbletone 158

FORGIVENESS
Not on Purpose 163

GOD'S LOVE AND CARE
Caught by the Tide 68
Jesus Knows and Cares 182
Mysterious Rider, The 101

GOD'S POWER IN CREATION
God's Plan for Our World 152
Our World in Space 141
People in Our World, The 148

GRANDPARENTS
Present for Grandma 174

HEALING
How Doris Lost Her Voice 29

HEAVEN AND NEW EARTH
God's Plan for Our World 152

HELPFULNESS
"I'm Here, Sir" 14

HONESTY
Honest Tommy 189

INFLUENCE
Little Shadow 77

JESUS, LOVE OF
Jesus Knows and Cares 182

KINDNESS
The Mysterious Rider 101

LOVE TO THOSE WHO NEED IT
They Gave Their Best 122

MISSIONS
Clouds at a Picnic 82

PERSISTENCE
Digging for a Bicycle 133
Richard's Rubbish Heap 9

PRAYERS, ANSWERS TO
Clouds at a Picnic 82

SECOND COMING, SIGNS OF
Flaming Beacons 36

SMOKING
Boy in Chains, A 19

TITHING
Four Times as Much 49

TOLERANCE
Frontiers of Peace 179

TRUTHFULNESS
Daddy's Birthday Present 117

WORK
How Terence Got His Train 88

7

Artists participating in the illustration of this volume are: Harry Anderson, Harry Baerg, Robert Berran, Fred Collins, Kreigh Collins, William Dolwick, Arlo Greer, John Gourley, Russ Harlan, Joseph Hennesy, William Hutchinson, Manning de V. Lee, Donald Muth, Vernon Nye, Herbert Rudeen, and Jack White. Cover by John Steel.

STORY **1**

Richard's Rubbish Heap

RICHARD WAS AS EXCITED as a dog with ten tails. He had always wanted to "invent" something and now he had done so. His big "fire balloon," on which he had been working for several weeks, was almost ready. There were just a few more odds and ends to fix, and then he would be able to set light to the wad of cotton set in a frame at the bottom and watch the big paper bag fill with hot air and soar away into the sky.

It was going to be a big day for him, for all his friends were coming to see the great sight. He had told them all about it long before he had even worked out the design, and he was sure their eyes would "pop out" when they saw it completed.

And it was something to see, too, I can tell you. Six feet high and four feet in diameter, it had been no small job to build. Richard had first made a framework of very light, strong wire. Then he had cut long strips of tissue paper, of various colors, all of the proper shape—like slices of orange peel—so that when pasted together they made a big paper globe around the wire frame. What a task it had been pasting

9

"It's lifting! It's lifting!" cried Richard excitedly as the big tissue-paper bag began to rise.

10   the edges of that paper! Often it had torn or got stuck in the wrong place!

At the very bottom of the frame there was a circle of wire, in the center of which, supported on two cross wires, was the pad of cotton soaked in fuel, which, at the right moment, was to be set alight to heat the air inside the balloon.

At last everything was ready for the grand ascent. All Richard's friends were standing around, waiting impatiently for the moment when the balloon would sail aloft.

Richard, however, was not in a hurry. He wanted to enjoy this moment of triumph to which he had looked forward so long and for which he had worked so hard. He kept explaining how he had designed the balloon and why he was sure it would rise into the air. Over and over again he answered all the questions the boys asked about it.

At last, with a great flourish, he applied a match to the

cotton. It flared up, and the children stood back to watch as the air inside became heated and the big tissue-paper bag gradually filled out.

"It's lifting!" cried Richard excitedly. "It's lifting! It's going up!"

He was clapping his hands for glee when a puff of wind blew the flame toward the tissue paper. There was no time to save it. In a moment the whole balloon had dropped to the ground in flames.

Poor Richard! Heartbroken, he ran indoors, eager to get away from his friends who had expected so much of him and his much-advertised "invention." He felt ashamed that he had said so much about it before it had been proved a success. And there was all the work he had put on it—all his spare time for weeks! Now there was nothing left but a heap of ashes and tangled wire.

That night Father found him in his bedroom. "Oh, why did it have to burn up?" moaned Richard.

Thomas A. Edison experimenting in his laboratory.

"Don't worry too much about it," said Father. "Much worse things happen in this old world. What really matters is not that the old balloon is all burned up but that you worked so hard trying to make something worthwhile."

"But it's all wasted," wailed Richard.

"No, not wasted," said Daddy. "Think of all you have learned—all that you have read about balloons, all the little tricks about bending wire and sticking tissue paper together. All that isn't lost. It will prove useful someday. You'll see.

"But I did so want to invent something," sobbed Richard.

"I know," said Father, "but worthwhile things don't get invented as quickly as that. Think of Edison and how long he experimented before he invented the electric light and the phonograph and the other things he gave the world. Do you think he discovered them all at once? No, indeed. He worked and worked over them, trying and failing and trying again."

"For weeks and weeks, as I did?" asked Richard.

"Yes, for years and years," comforted Father. "And he had so many failures that it is a wonder he carried on as he did. You should just see his rubbish heap."

"His rubbish heap?" questioned Richard in surprise.

"Yes, indeed," said Father. "I've heard that it is shown to all who visit one of his old workshops. Every time an experiment went wrong he would throw it out and start again. He didn't let failure discourage him, and neither must you. Build another balloon and a better one next time. Invent one that won't catch fire. Find out what was wrong and make it right. That's how all worthwhile inventions come about."

"I suppose that if Edison had a rubbish heap I shouldn't worry too much about my little pile of ashes," said Richard. "I'm going to start on a new balloon tomorrow."

"That's right," agreed Father. "That's the spirit that wins. Every real inventor has a rubbish heap, and you've made a good start toward success tonight."

"I'm Here, Sir!"

"MAURICE!" CRIED DADDY. "Come here, I want you to help me!"

There was no reply. Daddy went on with his work. A big load of firewood, ordered for next winter, had been dropped on the sidewalk, and he was hurrying to get it all in the woodshed before nightfall.

After a while he called again, but more insistently.

"Maurice! Where are you?"

Still no reply.

Daddy wondered whether he should leave the pile of wood and go in search of his son or continue with the job by himself. He decided to go on working.

In a little while, however, he began thinking about Maurice. "Why shouldn't the boy come and help?" he asked himself. Probably he was indoors in a comfortable armchair, reading.

He called again.

"Maurice! I'm waiting for you."

"Ye-ah," drawled a sleepy voice from somewhere in the house. "Did you call me?"

14

"Yes, I did call you," said Daddy. "Come and help carry this wood into the shed."

There was a long pause.

"Are you coming, Maurice," asked Daddy, "or shall I have to come and get you?"

"Aw, I suppose I'll have to come," said the sleepy voice. And in a few minutes Maurice, hands in pockets, came out the front door.

"What did you want me to do?" he asked.

"Surely you can see for yourself," said Daddy. "We must move this wood off the walk before nightfall. Come now, hurry up."

Maurice looked at the big pile, then began to lift the logs into the wheelbarrow for Daddy to wheel to the shed. He could work all right once he got going, but he badly needed a self-starter.

When the job was finished, and the last log had been carried in, Daddy turned to Maurice.

"Thanks, son," he said. "You're a great help. I like to have you working with me. If only you would come the first time you are called, you'd be perfect. I wonder whether you could improve along that line?"

"Aw, it's always hard to get started," said Maurice, "especially when I'm interested in something else."

"Let me tell you a story," said Daddy.

Maurice was "all ears" at once. He loved stories.

"Do you remember hearing or reading of a man called Shackleton—Sir Ernest Shackleton?"

"You mean the explorer who went to the South Pole?"

"Yes. Well, once when he was planning an expedition to the Antarctic he decided he must take someone called Wild with him, a man who had been a most faithful and devoted helper on former trips. But Wild was nowhere to be found. It was said that he had gone big-game hunting in the heart of

Africa, and there was no way to reach him.

" 'You had better give up trying to locate him,' said a friend. 'If he's in Africa you'll never find him. What's more, if he's big-game hunting he won't want to go to the Antarctic again anyway.'

" 'But I must have Wild along with me,' said Shackleton.

" 'Better sail without him,' said the friend. 'You can't find him, and even if you could, he wouldn't go.'

" 'If Wild knows I am going on this trip he will come,' said Shackleton. 'I'm sure he will, whether he is in Africa or anywhere else.'

" 'Don't fool yourself,' said his friend.

"Just then there was a knock on the door. It was a messenger boy with a card in his hand.

" 'There's a gentleman downstairs to see you, sir,' he said. 'Shall I bring him up?'

"Shackleton looked at the card.

"He read: 'Frank Wild.'

"It's Wild! He's here!' he cried. 'Bring him in.'

"Beaming with smiles, the old friends met and shook hands.

" 'But how, why——?' began Shackleton. 'I thought you were hunting big game in Africa.'

" 'I was, sir,' said Wild. 'But I heard you were going on this expedition, so I dropped everything and came at once.'

"Then, standing stiffly at attention and saluting, he said, 'I'm here, sir! Captain, what are your orders?'

18   "Now, Maurice, don't you think that Wild did a splendid thing? He didn't wait to be called. He just felt that he was needed and came along. He dropped everything he was doing and hurried to what he felt was his post of duty."

"That was grand of him," said Maurice.

"I wish——" began Daddy.

"I know," said Maurice.

He knew all right.

Next time Daddy called him to help on a job, a cheerful voice replied immediately:

"I'm here, sir! Captain, what are your orders?"

A Boy in Chains

THE OTHER DAY I saw a strange sight in New York City. Yes, it was a boy in chains.

"What!" you say, "a boy in chains nowadays?"

Yes, a real, live slave boy, despite the fact that Abraham Lincoln freed the slaves a long time ago.

The boy was quite small, which made me think that he was very young, but his face had a strange, oldish look, so that I couldn't tell just what his age might be. As I looked at him, I was struck with the fact that he was puffing away at a cigarette like a grownup. So I decided to speak to him.

"How is it that you are smoking at your age?" I asked him kindly.

"Can't help it, mister," he replied, with amazing frankness.

"Can't help it?" I repeated. "That's very strange. How old are you?"

"Just thirteen."

"Just thirteen!" I exclaimed. "Then how long have you been smoking?"

"Three years." 19

20   "Three years!" I said, astonished. "You mean to tell me you have been smoking since you were ten?"

"Yes. The other boys smoked, so I started too."

"What other boys?"

"All the boys in my grade at school. And most of the seventh-graders smoke too."

"And the sixth?"

"Yes, mister, some in the sixth. I know; I've seen them."

I was amazed, wondering how many boy slaves to the smoking habit there must be in the country nowadays.

"And now I suppose you can't give it up," I said.

"Right. I can't. I've tried, but it's no use."

"Then you're a slave," I said.

"That's about it. I am."

A slave at thirteen!

"You'll be terribly sorry later on," I said. "You are poisoning yourself. You will never be able to do well in play or in work if you go on like this."

"I know," he said. "Sort of gets your wind; you can't run so fast. I've felt it myself out on the school playground."

So he had noticed the terrible effect of tobacco already. At thirteen!

Poor little slave!

We talked on awhile about the harm that smoking does, and the importance of breaking the habit right away.

"You will have to call up all your will power," I said to

22 him, "and put your foot down now."

"Maybe after I have smoked these," he said, pointing to the big pack that was bulging from his pocket.

"No," I said firmly. "If you want to stop it there's only one time to do it."

"And that's now," he said with a smile. "I know."

That raised my hopes.

"You're right, son," I said. "You have the idea. Stop now, and throw the rest away. Will you?"

"I think I will," he said.

"Good boy!" I replied. "Promise me that you'll never touch the horrid things again."

"All right."

We shook hands on it, and I sent up a little prayer that Jesus would help him in the struggle he was bound to have.

As we parted there was a brave look on his face.

My little slave friend had come very near to freedom. His chains were unloosed.

Did he step out of them into a new life of liberty?

Did he keep his promise?

I rather think he did.

4

Tale of a Tangle

IT WAS HOLIDAY TIME, and the weather was good, and George wanted a kite.

It was not the only thing George wanted, by any means, but just for the moment it was the thing he wanted most.

"Dad," he said, "do come and look at the lovely kite they have in the corner store. It's just the one I want."

"I believe it," said Dad, not much interested.

"Do come and look at it," begged George.

"I've seen lots of kites," said Dad.

"But this is a new kind," persisted George, "and I've got to have it. And if we don't go soon it may be gone."

"Oh, don't be so impatient," replied Dad. "There's no great hurry."

"But there is, really. You see, someone will buy it if we don't. I saw a boy looking in the shop just now, and I'm sure he wanted it."

"Let him have it," said Dad.

"Oh, no, Dad," said George. "After all, it's only a dollar."

Dad pricked up his ears.

"Only a dollar? And who is going to pay for it?"

23

"Oh, I am, of course. That is—er—if you will lend me the dollar."

"Ah!" said Dad, "I seem to have heard that before."

George returned to the attack. He said that he had never had a kite in all his life, while other boys always had kites. Some had two or three. If he had a kite he would be very, very happy. He would never bother anyone again. Dad would be free to read his paper without any interruption. Dad would not be asked to fly the kite or wind in the string, unless he really wanted to do it. The kite would indeed become the greatest family boon that had ever been purchased. And all for a dollar, to be paid back, under solemn promise, in the next twelve months.

Convinced of George's good intentions, Dad at last gave in and found himself being led to the corner store.

"That's it, that's the one!" cried George. "It's still there.

I'm sure glad no one bought it while you were making up your mind, Dad."

"What a pity, you mean! By the way, it's rather small and very flimsy, isn't it?"

"Yes," admitted George. "A large one would really be better, but it would cost more money, you know."

"Yes, I see."

They discussed kites for twenty minutes with the lady in the store, after which Dad found himself the poorer by one dollar and fifty cents.

They had decided to take a larger kite, and the one dollar one was put back in the window.

George was delighted.

"I'll pay you back," he said eagerly.

"Yes, of course," said Dad, having a vision of the debt being spread over two years instead of one.

As they were leaving the store Dad noticed something.

"Where is your string?" he said.

"String?" repeated George.

"Yes, string," said Dad. "Got any?"

"Why—er—no," said George ruefully, "I—no—I really never thought about it. Don't they give the string with the kite?"

"Not usually. The string will cost you another seventy cents."

George's face fell. "I'm afraid I'll have to borrow that too," he said.

Dad laughed. "I'll give you that, too, son. But mind, whatever you do, don't undo that ball of string until you are ready to use it. Then wind it on a thick round piece of wood."

"Oh, I know what to do," said George. "I can do it all right."

They left the store and returned home. Dad had left two dollars and twenty cents there instead of a dollar.

At dinnertime there was no sign of George.

"George!" called Dad. "Where are you?"

Mother came in.

"It's all right," she said. "George is having a little trouble, but he'll be along soon."

But George did not come along soon. Dad went to find out what was the matter. He found him in the next room with the ball of string on the floor. To be more correct, it was a *pile* of string. Indeed, it was one heartbreaking tangle. Poor George sat on the floor beside it, picking, pulling, twisting, winding, his face meanwhile the very picture of gloom.

"What does this mean?" asked Dad. "Is that the lovely ball of string we bought this morning?"

George turned his tear-filled eyes upward and looked into his father's face. Then without saying a word he returned to his seemingly unending task.

"George, how did this happen?" asked Dad. "Did you undo the ball before you were ready to wind it on the stick?"

◀ Painting by Russell Harlan

Daddy found George on the floor with a pile of string around him in a hopeless tangle.

28 George nodded, and the nod threw a tear out on the floor.

"Well," said Dad, "that was very disobedient of you. You are an impatient boy, George, and you deserve to be punished."

"I am," said George.

As for a tangle, well, Mother had a go at it, Auntie had a go at it, Sister had a go at it, and, of course, Dad had a go at it; and it was not until two days later that Dad's one dollar and fifty cents soared into the air at the end of that ball of string.

Now every time George sees a kite in the sky he remembers his mistakes and makes up his mind never to repeat them.

How Doris Lost
Her Voice

DORIS WAS A LITTLE GIRL just seven years old when a dreadful thing happened to her. She was a bright little girl and was getting along so well at school that Mother was very proud of her.

But Doris had one bad fault—she always wanted her own way no matter what Mother said to her. Sometimes she would say, "Yes, Mother," and then go away and do whatever she pleased, instead.

This problem came up about the way Doris was to go to school. Mother wanted her to go one way, and Doris wanted to go another way, so there was a good deal of trouble in the home.

"Darling," said Mother one morning, "I wish you wouldn't take that short cut along the back streets. Sometimes the boys get very rough down there, and I don't want anything to happen to you. Please keep to the main streets, and then everything will be all right."

"But, Mother," pleaded Doris, "those back streets are quite all right. I've looked down them so many times, and they are almost always empty. It would save me such a lot of

29

30   time if I could walk to school that way."

"It wouldn't save you more than five minutes altogether," said Mother, "and I would rather you would take a little more time and be safe."

"Well, I don't see why I shouldn't go that way," said Doris in a grumbly tone of voice.

"Maybe not," said Mother, "but, mind, I want you to keep to the main streets."

Doris, pouting a little, went off to school. And because Mother's words were fresh in her memory, she went to school the long way round. But in the afternoon, when she was coming home, she began to think that she was right, not Mother.

"I can't see why Mom doesn't want me to go home the short way," she said to herself. "Mom just doesn't understand. If she were a little girl as tired and hungry as I am, she'd take the short cut; I know she would."

So she argued with herself until she felt convinced that the short cut would be quite all right this afternoon.

It was. There was hardly anybody in the streets, and

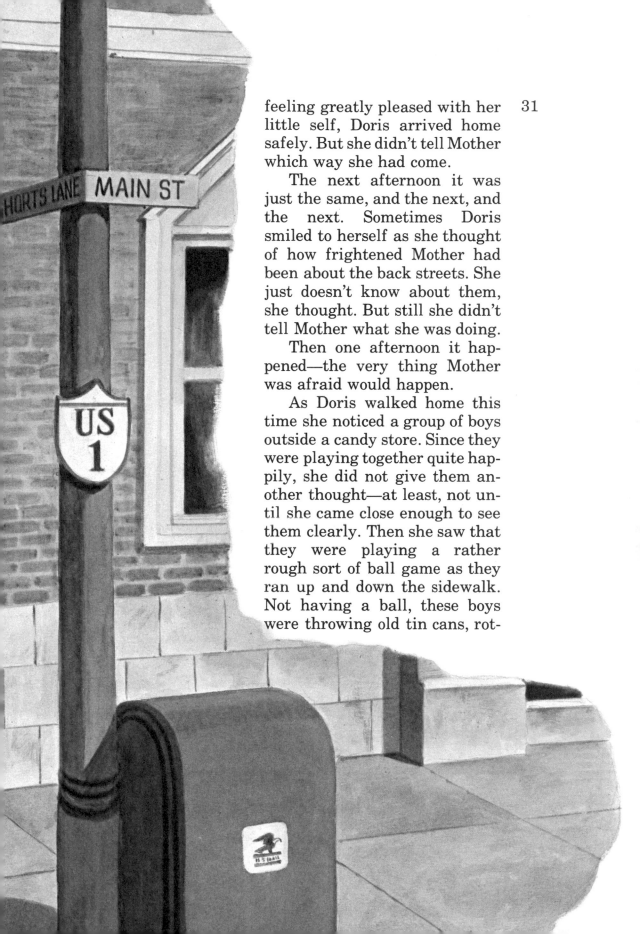

feeling greatly pleased with her 31
little self, Doris arrived home
safely. But she didn't tell Mother
which way she had come.

The next afternoon it was
just the same, and the next, and
the next. Sometimes Doris
smiled to herself as she thought
of how frightened Mother had
been about the back streets. She
just doesn't know about them,
she thought. But still she didn't
tell Mother what she was doing.

Then one afternoon it happened—the very thing Mother
was afraid would happen.

As Doris walked home this
time she noticed a group of boys
outside a candy store. Since they
were playing together quite hap-
pily, she did not give them another thought—at least, not until she came close enough to see
them clearly. Then she saw that
they were playing a rather
rough sort of ball game as they
ran up and down the sidewalk.
Not having a ball, these boys
were throwing old tin cans, rot-

ten cabbages, and tomatoes—in fact, anything they could pick up.

Suddenly they spied Doris, who had moved
for safety to the opposite side of the street.
"Get her!" they cried. And they began to throw
things at her just as hard as they could.

Doris began to run, but it was no use. The
boys could run as fast as she. Soon they were chasing her
down the street like a pack of wolves, each one hurling at her
whatever he could pick up, all the time shouting, "Hit her!
Hit her!"

Poor little Doris could not get away, and soon her pretty
dress was a terrible sight!

Of course, nobody meant to hurt her, but suddenly she
gave a scream, clutched her throat, and fell over into the
street.

The boys crowded round, wondering what had happened.

"Her throat is bleeding," said one of the bigger boys.
"Somebody must have thrown a stone."

Somebody had, but no one would say who; and after all, what was the use of bothering about that now? The mischief had been done.

They tried to get Doris to say what was the matter, but she didn't reply. She couldn't. Then the boys became really frightened, and one of them ran for a policeman. He picked Doris up in his strong arms and carried her home.

"Doris! What's the matter?" cried Mother, as she opened the door. "Doris! What has happened?"

Still Doris could not speak.

Mother, talking to her all the time, took her indoors and bathed her throat; but Doris never said a word. She seemed to be trying to speak, but couldn't. Now Mother became very much frightened and took her to the doctor. When he examined her he said that the stone had struck her voice box and maybe she would never be able to talk again.

Some days later they both went to see a specialist, and he said just what the doctor had said. They came away from his office feeling very, very sad.

Doris would never be able to speak anymore! Do you wonder that when Mother was all alone, she cried and cried? Well, she did. And Doris thought—oh, how often!—how foolish she had been not to take Mother's advice. What a price she had paid for her disobedience!

Months passed. The wound on Doris' throat healed, but

she was still unable to say a word. By this time Mother had begun to believe that she would never hear the dear, sweet voice of her little girl again.

Then one day there was a knock at the front door. Mother went to open it and found a man selling books.

"No," she said. "Not today, thank you."

"But they are children's books," he said. "Maybe you have a little boy or girl——"

Then Mother thought of Doris and invited the man to step inside.

As soon as the man saw Doris he brought out some of his books—among them *Uncle Arthur's Bedtime Stories*—and began talking to her about them. He asked Doris what she thought of the pictures, but there was no reply. Surprised, he turned to Mother, but she merely put her finger on her lips and shook her head.

"Oh, I'm so sorry," said the man. "I didn't understand. Isn't there any hope?"

"None," said Mother. "None at all. We have tried every

doctor and every specialist we know."

"There is someone else who might help," said the man.

"Who is it?" asked Mother eagerly.

"The Great Physician. Have you tried Jesus?"

"No," said Mother, hanging her head a little. "We haven't."

"Would you mind if I were to ask Him?" asked the man.

"No, of course not," said Mother, "if you wish."

So the stranger got down on his knees beside Doris and prayed—oh, so simply—that Jesus, in His great love, would make her better and give her back her voice if He so willed.

Then he arose from his knees and said good-by, promising to bring back the books Mother had ordered.

A surprise awaited him when he returned a week later.

As he approached Doris' house, he saw a little girl running to meet him as fast as her legs would carry her.

"We are so glad you have come!" she cried, taking his hand in hers. "We have been waiting all week for you."

"My dear!" he exclaimed. "Do I really hear you speak?"

"Oh, yes! Yes!" she cried. "It happened just as you left. I ran after you to tell you, but you were too far away."

There were tears in all their eyes as they talked over this wonderful thing that had happened and thanked the great Lover of children for what He had done for Doris.

Flaming Beacons

THAT WAS A WONDERFUL night, May 6, 1935, when the people of England celebrated the Silver Jubilee of King George V with a great bonfire.

Crowning all the various celebrations of that day, the bonfire was lighted in Hyde Park by the king himself.

Even now I seem to see the flames of that towering beacon leaping heavenward, piercing the darkness with long tongues of fire, and lighting up the faces of the thousands upon thousands of people who had gathered in the area to watch the blaze.

As the king sat in his palace and pressed the button that lighted this colossal bonfire, hundreds of other beacons were kindled throughout the country. From hill to hill they flashed the joyful message that King George had been spared to reign for twenty-five years.

All over the country, people climbed the highest peaks to see the beacons blaze. Some counted more than thirty.

Whether one or many, I am sure every boy and girl who saw them will never forget the sight. There's something so romantic about a beacon. It makes you think of days of long

36

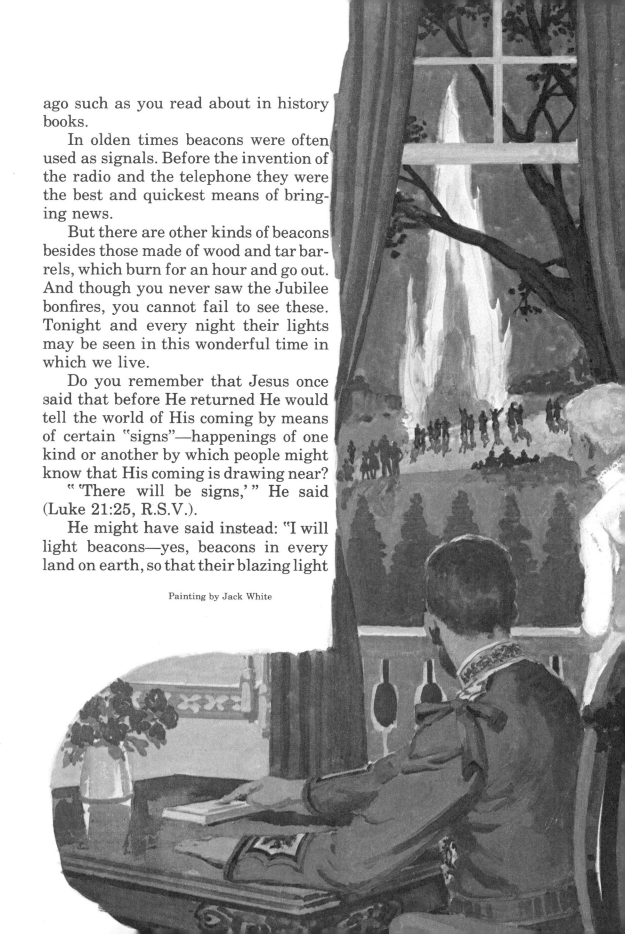

ago such as you read about in history books.

In olden times beacons were often used as signals. Before the invention of the radio and the telephone they were the best and quickest means of bringing news.

But there are other kinds of beacons besides those made of wood and tar barrels, which burn for an hour and go out. And though you never saw the Jubilee bonfires, you cannot fail to see these. Tonight and every night their lights may be seen in this wonderful time in which we live.

Do you remember that Jesus once said that before He returned He would tell the world of His coming by means of certain "signs"—happenings of one kind or another by which people might know that His coming is drawing near?

" 'There will be signs,' " He said (Luke 21:25, R.S.V.).

He might have said instead: "I will light beacons—yes, beacons in every land on earth, so that their blazing light

Painting by Jack White

shall let everybody know that the hour of My return is at hand."

Those promised beacons have been lighted. If you care to look for them you will see them flaming all about you.

Look at the marvelous inventions we see today—planes that fly faster than sound; rockets that travel thousands of miles; spacecraft that carry men to the moon and instruments to other planets. What are these but signs that we are living in "the time of the end"? Every one is a flaming beacon, telling that Jesus is coming soon.

Look at the terrible fear of the future that is coming into people's hearts as they think about atomic bombs. Surely this is the very " 'distress of nations in perplexity,' " which Jesus said would prevail just before His return (Luke 21:25, R.S.V.).

Look at the wonderful way the gospel of Jesus

H. BAERG

...ME AGAIN

is being preached in all the world today. Was there ever such missionary activity before? Never. And Jesus said that when His gospel has been preached in all the world as a witness unto all nations, then "the end" will come (Matthew 24:14). So this is another beacon, and there are many more like them—flaming beacons in every land, bearing the message to all people that the coming of the Lord draws near.

What should they mean to us? Surely this—that we should make certain that we have given our hearts to Him. If we have, there's nothing to worry about. To His children, the thought of His coming is altogether happy.

For it will not be a different Jesus who will descend from the skies in glory, but "this same Jesus" who lived in the Holy Land in the long ago and took little children into His arms to bless

HARRY BAERG, ARTIST

40 them, and said, " 'Let the children come to me, . . . for to such belongs the kingdom of God' " (Mark 10:14, R.S.V.).

When He comes again He will be just as kind, just as loving, just as friendly, just as sympathetic, as He ever was, only crowned as "King of kings, and Lord of lords."

Through the centuries there have been many times when people have mistakenly expected Jesus to come on a certain date, and He has not come. Many others, impatient at His delay, have ceased to watch and wait. They have gone away saying, "He will never come; why wait any longer?"

But others who love the Lord have pressed into the crowd to take the places of the disheartened ones, so that today there are people all around the world looking up, waiting.

One day Jesus will come. Nobody knows the day or the hour, but the promised signs, the blazing of the beacons of prophecy, seem to tell us that we shall not have to wait very long now before we shall see our King.

And then? Will you cheer? Will you be glad to see Him?

I hope so, for He is coming back to gather His children to Himself, to take them to their glorious heavenly home, where all will be joy and happiness forevermore. He has wonderful plans in mind for all who love Him, plans that will amaze and delight them through all the years to come.

So we must be ready when He comes, "waiting and watching for Him." Yes, and ready to say with a cheer when we see the first sign of His appearing: " 'Lo, this is our God; we have waited for him, that he might save us. This is the Lord; . . . let us be glad and rejoice in his salvation' " (Isaiah 25:9, R.S.V.).

Then what a jubilee there will be! What a day of rejoicing for all who love Him!

7

Peter and the Pumpkin Seed

"MOTHER," SAID PETER one day, "I wish I could earn some money."

"Well, dear," said Mother, "aren't you earning money now? You help me with little jobs, and I give you some money every week."

"Yes, I know," said Peter. "But I mean some *real* money, like the grown-up people get. Wages, you know, Mother."

"Oh, well, you will earn wages, I hope, when you grow up," said Mother. "There's time enough for that."

"But I want to earn some now," insisted Peter. "Couldn't I go over to Mr. Johnson's farm and work for him?"

"Well, I suppose you could, if he would give you work. But you are only a little boy yet, you know. I doubt that he would be bothered with you."

"But won't you ask him?" pleaded Peter. "Just ask him. He can only say No."

At long last, after much persuasion, Mother promised to see what she could do about it. Next day she talked to Farmer Johnson, and he agreed that Peter could spend one week of his vacation on the farm, working each morning for an

41

agreed sum, with play in the afternoon if he did his work well.

Peter surely felt grown-up when he set off with his little bag containing his pajamas, hairbrush, toothbrush, and other things he needed to go to work for the first time in his life.

Farmer Johnson gave him a cheery welcome and set him to work at once doing odd jobs around the house.

Then one morning when the time came to begin to work, Farmer Johnson told Peter that he had a very special task for him that day.

"Peter," he said, "I want you to give me some real help this morning. Will you do something very important, and do it just as I say?"

"Oh, yes," said Peter, all excited. "Of course I will. What is it?"

"Come along with me," said Farmer Johnson, "and you will soon find out."

First of all they went through the farmyard, where Farmer Johnson picked up a two-gallon pail full of pumpkin seed. Then together they walked out to one of the fields, which was all ready for planting.

Peter wasn't quite sure what it was all about, but guessed that his job would have something to do with that seed. Maybe he would have to carry the pail while Farmer Johnson planted it.

"Now look," said Farmer Johnson. "Do you see this field?"

"Yes," said Peter meekly. As he spoke he thought he had never seen such a big field in all his life.

"Well, now, I want you to plant these pumpkin seeds in this field, and I want it done very carefully."

"You mean me?" said Peter, not sure he had heard correctly.

"Yes, you," said Farmer Johnson. "I want you to walk down this first furrow and every ten paces put in three seeds and cover them with earth. Then when you reach the end of the first row, move over to the next row and work your way back. Go on until the pail is empty."

"Yes, Mr. Johnson," said Peter, proud to have a real job at last.

"You understand just how I want it done?"

"Yes, three seeds in each hole and ten paces between holes."

"That's a good boy," said Farmer Johnson, with a smile playing around his weatherbeaten face. "I think I'll be going now. Oh, by the way, as soon as you have finished you can go and have a swim."

"Oh, thank you, Mr. Johnson," said Peter eagerly. "I won't be long."

"I wonder!" said Farmer Johnson to himself, as he left and went to his other tasks.

Meanwhile Peter set to work in earnest.

"Three seeds, ten paces—three seeds, ten paces," he said.

44   Then he murmured to himself, as he moved slowly down the long row: *"Three seeds.* Then one, two, three, four, five, six, seven, eight, nine, ten, *three seeds.* One, two, three, four, five, six, seven, eight, nine, ten, *three seeds . . ."*

At last he reached the end of the row and turned eagerly to look back to where he began. He could hardly see the spot, it was so far away.

Then he looked at his pail, and his heart sank.

It seemed just as full as when he began!

"Why," he said to himself, "I've put in all those seeds, and yet it seems as though I haven't used any. I'll have to work harder still if I am ever going to get that swim."

So he moved over to the next furrow and began his long, slow journey back to where he began. Again it was three seeds—ten paces—three seeds—ten paces.

Finally the second row was finished, and once more he looked at his pail. He felt like crying. Truly the level of the seed had gone down a little, but, oh, so little!

He was getting just a wee bit tired now, and more than a wee bit hot, and as he looked at the huge pile of seed yet to be

planted he told himself that he never would get that swim
Farmer Johnson had promised him if he continued this way.

Just then a very naughty thought came into his mind.

"I wonder whether it would matter," he said to himself, "if I were to put in four or perhaps five seeds each time? That would get the pail emptied much faster. And Farmer Johnson would never know about it, not when the seeds are covered over."

He thought about it awhile, looked up at the sun, felt himself getting hotter and hotter, thought again of the swimming pool, and decided to do it.

Now his rate was five seeds—ten paces—five seeds—ten paces.

At last he came to the end of the third row, and turning, worked his way back to finish the fourth. But, alas, even then the pail seemed almost as full as before.

Tired and discouraged, Peter sat down.

"He shouldn't have given me such a big job to do," he said to himself. "He must have known I never could plant all this seed and still have a swim. He didn't mean for me to have a

swim at all. I know he didn't. But I can't tell him that I couldn't finish the job. I'll go on and on and on till—but let me see, if it was all right to put five seeds in, why shouldn't I put in six or seven?"

And that is what Peter did, all up and down the next two rows.

Ten paces—seven seeds—ten paces—seven seeds. The task seemed endless.

It was getting late now, and even seven seeds in a hole didn't seem to empty the pail any faster.

"I don't care," said Peter to himself. "I'm going to empty this pail whatever I do, and I'm going to have my swim. I'll put a whole handful of seeds in every time."

He started off once more, tired and ill-tempered. And this time it was ten paces—handful—ten paces—handful.

At this rate, of course, the pail was soon emptied. With great relish Peter turned it upside down and hurried away to the swimming pool.

But somehow the swim was no fun at all. He had a strange, uncomfortable feeling inside. Just what it was, or why it was, he could not say. But it was there, just the same.

Farmer Johnson hailed him and asked whether he had finished the job.

"Oh, yes," called Peter, "all done." But again that strange feeling bothered him.

"Good for you," said Farmer Johnson; but the words didn't

do Peter half the good they usually did.

That night he went home. Mother asked him how he had enjoyed himself, and he said, "All right." But inside he felt that it was not all right. He kept worrying about those pumpkin seeds. And suddenly it dawned on him that they would all come up!

Until that moment he had never thought about that. Of course they would come up! He went hot and cold all over. Then he got on his knees beside his bed and asked God to kill some of the seeds, and not let them grow.

But they were growing even as he prayed. In a few days they were all above ground.

Just then Farmer Johnson took a little walk to find out why it was that Peter had finished his job so much sooner than he had expected him to.

He smiled, a strange little understanding smile.

They didn't meet again—Peter and Farmer Johnson—until the next time they went to church.

48   Now, it so happened that Farmer Johnson went in one door and Peter went in the other door, and suddenly, right in the middle of the aisle, they came face to face.

Peter thought it was the day of judgment. If he could have done so he would have turned and run, but something kept him riveted to the spot. He could see nothing but Farmer Johnson and behind him millions of pumpkin plants. His lip began to quiver.

Farmer Johnson saw and understood, perfectly. He had a kind heart, and he knew at once that Peter had learned his lesson.

"Don't cry," he whispered, as he came very close to Peter's ear. "Just remember that the seeds you sow in life always come up. 'Whatsoever a man soweth, that shall he also reap.' "

He squeezed Peter's hand in forgiveness, and Peter wished that he could walk out of church right then and there and plant that field all over again.

8

Four Times as Much

JOHN HAD BEEN TAUGHT to give God a tithe, one tenth of all the money he earned. It is a noble thing to do, and the Bible says that people who follow this plan with their money may always be sure of receiving a special blessing from Heaven.

From the very first time that John had earned any money of his own, he had most carefully set aside one tenth for the Lord. This he had put in the collection plate at church. If he received fifty cents for running an errand, then he saved five cents for God. If he received a dollar for helping to wash somebody's car, then he put ten cents aside in the same way.

Year by year he continued to divide his money like this, but as he grew older and noticed that his school friends had lots of things he couldn't afford to buy, he began to leave God out sometimes. He didn't tell Mother, of course, because he knew she would be disappointed; and so that he wouldn't feel too bad about it himself, he wrote down in a little book all he knew he should pay God and didn't. He told himself that someday, when he made more money, he would pay it all up.

Of course that day did not come. It never does. And so the   49

◀ Vernon Nye, Artist

figure in John's little notebook grew larger and larger, and the possibility of his ever paying it became more and more remote.

Then one day he came home from school all excited with the news that a very special outing had been planned. His teacher had arranged for a wonderful trip into the country, where they would have boat rides and good things to eat—and great fun. The only difficulty was the expense. It was going to cost three dollars each.

"Well," said Mother, "I couldn't pay even that. If you want to go very badly you will have to use some of your own money."

John's face fell. He did so want to go with all the others in his class, but how could he use any more of his money when he owed God so much already?

Going upstairs, he opened the drawer where he kept his pennies and the little account book and began to count up to see how much he still had left.

"Twenty-five cents, fifty cents, a dollar, one dollar and fifty cents, one dollar and seventy-five cents, two dollars."

So he counted.

"Two dollars and fifty cents, two dollars and seventy-five cents, three dollars."

He had enough, just enough. He could go to the picnic after all!

But then he noticed the little notebook. Opening it slowly, he began counting again. And the more he counted, the more his heart sank.

Could it be possible he owed God so much?

One dollar, two dollars, three dollars!

Dreadful thought! If he paid God all he owed Him he would have nothing left. Then he could not possibly go to the picnic. What should he do?

He was getting into a terrible state of mind when the door opened softly and Mother entered. Quickly he threw his money and book into the drawer and closed it.

But somehow Mother guessed what was the matter. Mother usually does guess right, doesn't she?

Sitting down on John's bed, Mother picked up his Bible and turned the pages slowly until she came to the third chapter of the book of Malachi. And there she read those old familiar words: "Will man rob God? Yet you are robbing me. But you say, 'How are we robbing thee?' In your tithes and offerings. . . . Bring the full tithes into the storehouse, that there may be food in my house; and thereby put me to the test, says the Lord of hosts, if I will not open the windows of heaven for you and pour down for you an overflowing blessing" (Malachi 3:8-10, R.S.V.).

John had heard Mother read these verses many times, but somehow this time they made a deeper impression on his mind than ever before.

"Mother," he said, "I've decided not to go to that picnic."

"You have, dear?" said Mother. "Why?"

"Well, I might as well tell you. I have just three dollars saved up, and I owe it all to God. I haven't paid my tithe since

52   I don't know when, and I'm going to pay it now instead of going to the picnic. I'll be disappointed, but I wish you would take this money, so that I won't be tempted to spend it."

John passed over his precious three dollars to Mother, who, for a moment, hardly knew what to say.

"I think," she said after a pause, "I think you have made the right decision, John, and I am sure that somehow it will come out right. God does such wonderful things, you know, when we try to please Him. And when He opens the windows of heaven, He usually opens them wide."

The next few days were hard days for John. It seemed as though every few minutes some boy or girl would ask him whether he was going to the picnic, and he would have to

reply, "No, not this time." And then he would be asked, "Why not? What's the matter? Are you sick? Is your mother ill? Don't you want to go?" And he would have to try to explain without really telling them anything.

At last the day arrived. This, thought John, would be the hardest day of all—to see everybody going away and have to stay behind himself.

And then, early that very morning, the postman called. He had a letter for John. It was from a relative living in the West Indies. Inside was a check for twelve dollars—exactly four times as much as the tithe John had given to God. John went to the outing after all. Indeed, he was the happiest boy there. The windows of heaven had opened again, wide as the love of God.

STORY **9**

One Naughty Lamb

IF YOU HAVE EVER been to New Zealand you will remember the sheep. Thousands of them. Sheep all over the hills. Sheep all over the mountains. And sheep on the highways.

Sheep, of course, have the right of way. There's nothing you can do about them anyway. When you come across a flock of sheep on the road you just stop your car and wait for them to go by.

I was told that a good shepherd can tell at a glance exactly

how many sheep are in his flock. Maybe he can. But I couldn't tell how many there were in the flock that I came across on the road from Christchurch to Dunedin. Whether it was two thousand or three thousand I'll never know. There just seemed to be sheep everywhere, as far as I could see.

They were in the care of two shepherds and one dog—or I should say one dog and two shepherds—for the dog seemed to be doing all the work.

You should have seen that dog! He seemed to be everywhere at the same time, rushing this way and that, keeping his eyes on every single sheep, making sure that none strayed or got out of line.

As the flock drew near to our waiting car, it turned left onto a side road that led to new pastureland up in the green hills.

I thought to myself, Surely some of these sheep will walk straight on and miss the turn. No indeed. Not with that dog around. Like a flash he was right there, barking and nudging the sheep into the side road.

So the hundreds and hundreds of sheep passed by, right in front of me, a sight I will never forget.

56 As I watched, I thought how good these sheep were, all doing exactly as they were told, with not a single one giving any trouble. Wouldn't it be wonderful, I thought, if children would always behave like this!

But the sheep weren't all good, after all.

As the last of the sheep turned off the main highway onto the side road, and as drivers of waiting cars were starting their motors ready to go again, a small lamb suddenly turned and ran back toward the highway.

He came between the cars and headed down the road along which the flock had just come.

Maybe he thought that, seeing he had been at the back of the flock, nobody would notice if he ran away. With the dog so busy up front, this was his chance.

But the dog with a quick movement surprised him.

How that dog saw that one naughty lamb I'll never know.
But he did. And in far less time than it takes to tell about it he had headed off the lamb and turned him back toward the flock. When the lamb hesitated and balked, the dog moved closer, and you should have seen the look on his face! It was enough to frighten anybody.

At last the lamb was back with the flock, the shepherds followed them with their game little dog, and the cars moved on the highway again.

As we went on our way I kept thinking of that one naughty lamb and how he is like some children I know.

That boy in school who is always "cutting up" and bothering the teacher. That girl who is always wanting her own way, bucking Mother's plans for her and causing a lot of trouble. Have you ever seen anybody like this?

Could that naughty little lamb be *you?*

The Story
of Flight

HAVE YOU EVER wished you could fly like the birds? King David did, for once he said, " 'O that I had wings like a dove.' " (Psalm 55:6, R.S.V.).

Long before airplanes were thought of many people made all sorts of attempts to fly. Usually they fastened large wings to their arms and then jumped off some high wall or hillside in the hope that by moving their arms they would be able to fly. Needless to say, all these early attempts ended in failure.

In the year 1782 two brothers named Montgolfier, living at Annonay, near Lyons, France, hit upon a bright idea. They had been watching the movements of the clouds, and it suddenly occurred to them that if they could shut up something like a cloud in a large, light bag, it might rise and carry the bag with it into the air.

Accordingly, they made a large bag and held it over a fire until it was filled with smoke. To their surprise and delight, the bag rose into the air. Of course, they thought it was the smoke that raised the bag, and it was not until some time afterward that they learned it was the heated air and not the smoke that worked the "miracle" for them.

58

Over and over the two brothers tried their experiment, until, at last, encouraged by their success, they decided to make a very large balloon and have a public ascent. On the 5th of June, 1783, they took their balloon into a wide open space and inflated it over a fire. When released it rose rapidly to a great height, remaining in the air about ten minutes, and descending a mile and a half away.

The onlookers were thrilled, and the news spread far and wide. Nothing like this had ever happened before. A public collection was taken up to pay the expense of repeating the experiment.

The first air travelers were a sheep, a cock, and a duck. Enclosed in a cage and fastened to one of the Montgolfiers' balloons, they were sent up in the presence of the king and queen of France on the 19th of September, 1783. They remained in the air at a considerable height for eight minutes, and after descending were found to be none the worse for the

experience, except that the right wing of the cock had been hurt by the sheep.

It was nearly a month after this that the first human being made an ascent. This was a Frenchman named Rozier, who trusted himself to a captive balloon on the 15th of October, 1783. He repeated the experiment several times and demonstrated that it was possible to take a fire up with the balloon to keep it inflated. By the 21st of November he had developed enough confidence to risk going up in a free fire balloon, in which he drifted about for some time and descended safely.

The craze for ballooning spread from France to England, where the first balloon sent up was about ten feet in diameter and filled with hydrogen gas. It was inflated in London on November 25, 1783, and created great excitement.

Early the following year, a balloon just half this size was sent up in Kent and chanced to be the first one to cross the English Channel, being blown as far as Warneton in French Flanders.

Six months after this Scotland saw its first balloon ascent. Hundreds of people watched as a Mr. Tytler went up in a fire balloon from Edinburgh.

While Mr. Tytler was experimenting in Scotland, a man

named Vincent Lunardi was preparing for a personal ascent in London. His balloon was the talk of England, and excitement ran high. An immense crowd assembled to watch the ascent.

Lunardi took up a pigeon and a cat. The balloon itself was fitted with oars, with which he hoped to guide it. The pigeon escaped, and one of the oars broke off. A woman, seeing the oar falling, and thinking it was Lunardi, collapsed from shock, and died shortly afterward.

At that time a court was in session, trying an important case; but when the balloon came in sight the jury hastily gave a verdict of "Not guilty" and rushed out to see the sight. The king was in council, but the discussion was immediately broken up when the balloon appeared.

Crossing the English Channel for the first time proved an exciting

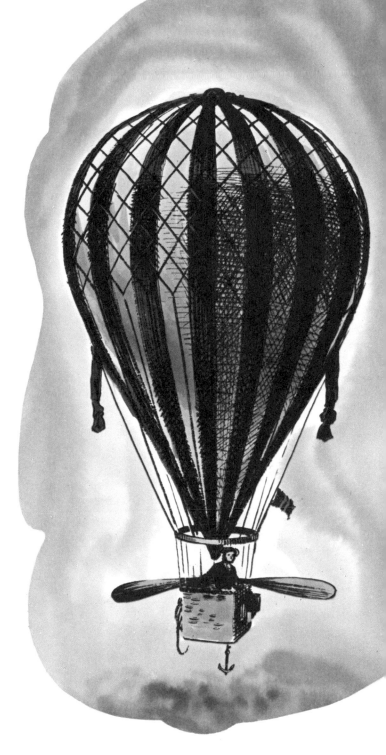

Lunardi made a balloon ascent over London about 1784.

experience for two pioneers, Dr. John Jeffries and Jean Pierre Blanchard. They left Dover on the 7th of January, 1785. When about a third of the way across, they found themselves descending and threw out everything they could. The balloon rose, but again began to descend while there was still a quarter of the way to go. Nearing the water, they decided to strip and throw out their clothes. This was done, and the balloon rose again. They were carried over the French coast, descending later in the Forest of Guinnes, nearly frozen but happy. Their fame spread everywhere.

Since those early days some very large balloons have been built. In 1836 one that was sent up from London traveled 480 miles and landed at Nassau in Germany, after a flight of 18 hours. It became known as the *Great Nassau* balloon, and after being brought back to England was used for several more ascents.

In 1863 a small cottage made of wickerwork was attached to a huge balloon. Two stories high, it contained "a small printing office, a photographic department, a refreshment room, lavatory, et cetera," according to the official report.

The little house held thirteen persons and enough food for a long voyage. But the voyage ended after only two hours because of an accident.

Fourteen days later, however, another ascent was made, and this time the balloon stayed up for seventeen hours and traveled 400 miles. Descending, it was caught in a strong wind and dragged over the ground. All its occupants were injured.

From the day that the first balloon went up, inventors tried to think of some means to propel them through the air so that they would not be at the mercy of the wind.

All sorts of paddles and oars were taken up, but to no purpose. Even light steam engines were used to drive propellers,

An early dirigible of the Zeppelin type.

but they were too dangerous, a spark from the fire being enough to blow the gas-filled balloon to pieces. One inventor, as late as 1872, took up eight laborers to turn a propeller for him, but he was unable to travel against the wind.

It was the invention of the gasoline engine that finally solved the problem of propelling balloons in the air. These engines combine great power with little weight and so are most suitable for such work. First attempts with them were not all successful, however, and there were several serious accidents. A gasoline engine taken up by a Dr. Wolfert in 1897 caused an explosion, and the doctor was killed.

Count Ferdinand von Zeppelin began his experiments in the year 1897. His plan was to make a long balloon supported by an aluminum framework and driven by engines. His first invention was tested in 1900, when it flew three and a half miles in ten minutes. Improvements followed, and during the first world war his *zeppelins* flew long

distances on important missions.

Other large and powerful airships crossed and recrossed the Atlantic. But so many of those monster airships crashed that no more are being made.

Then, too, heavier-than-air machines proved to be much safer and faster. Today it is hard to believe that when the twentieth century dawned there wasn't a machine in existence that could rise with its own power and carry a man with it. It was not, indeed, until the Wright brothers in 1903 made their large box kite—for that is what it resembled—and fitted it with a gasoline engine, that the first airplane made a successful flight.

Of course, there had been many experiments before this time, and scores of flying models had been made.

The great trouble was the lack of a powerful engine, light enough to be carried up with the machine. Steam engines were tried, but the weight of boiler, water, and fuel was far too great. Almost immediately after the gaso-

line engine had been invented, it was tried in flying machines. The gasoline engine was really the secret of the Wright brothers' success in their historic flight at Kitty Hawk, North Carolina, as it was of all later flights by other airmen.

With this difficulty overcome, great strides were soon made in airplane construction and achievement.

During the first world war, planes took part in both attack and defense, and this led to very rapid progress. In 1927 Charles Lindbergh made the first solo nonstop flight across the Atlantic.

In the second world war, air power became the deciding factor in the outcome. At the close of the war jet engines were being developed. Commercial planes became more and more important in long-distance shipping and travel.

◄ Painting by Harry Baerg

The Wright brothers making their first successful airplane flight in 1903 at Kitty Hawk, North Carolina.

Today air mail and air freight services reach almost any land, and jet planes carrying more than three hundred passengers cross continents and oceans. You can take off from Boston and fly eastward around the globe on a regular airline flight that will put you back in Boston less than 60 hours later.

And the end is not yet. On the one hand, supersonic airliners—traveling faster than sound—are being developed, and on the other hand helicopters and small private planes are being used more than ever before. Who knows—perhaps one day boys and girls will fly to school.

Youngsters who nowadays fly model planes often dream

of some day piloting great jet liners, and some of them even dream of going on other kinds of flight, far beyond our air-space flight into earth orbit or to the moon and beyond.

Best of all, everyone who loves Jesus supremely and is ready to meet Him when He comes again can go with Him on a space flight to the heaven of heavens, where God's throne is.

Caught by
the Tide

I HAVE TOLD so many stories about all sorts of boys and girls that perhaps it is time I told one about myself.

In my Bible, beside a certain text, are written three words, "North Uist Ford," and every time I look at them they bring back to my mind my most exciting adventure.

Many years ago—I won't tell you how many—when I was 15 years old, I decided to go to a missionary college. In order to obtain the necessary money I arranged with a certain publishing house—one that has since printed millions of copies of *Bedtime Stories*—to sell their Bible books during the summer.

They didn't seem to worry much about my age and sent me to the Outer Hebrides, off the west coast of Scotland. There I soon found myself, all alone, riding my bicycle over the barren, wind-swept islands. Day after day I knocked on cottage doors, trying my best to interest people in the books I carried.

For some weeks I lived in Stornoway, riding out every day right across the island to the villages on the other side. What

a weary journey that was—twelve miles without a house in sight, and sometimes with rain and wind beating in my face all the way. I traveled a little farther each day, until I had worked right up to the lighthouse at the most northerly point. The lighthouse keeper, by the way, was a very kind man. I remember him well, because he bought a book from me!

After doing all I could on the island of Lewis, I went by boat down to the next island, called North Uist, and found lodgings in a little thatched cottage, where the rats played around my bed at night.

There is a circular road on this island, and I rode and trudged all around it, going to many strange places where I am sure no boy of my age had ever tried to sell books before.

At last this island, too, was finished, and I wondered what to do next. So I began to explore southward, having been told that I could cross to the next island by walking across the ford at low tide. I liked this idea very much because walking across would save me the expense of hiring a boatman or taking a steamer.

70   Going down to the ford one morning, I looked it over very carefully. The tide was out, and from a distance it seemed that all I had to do was to walk straight across the sand to a little island, then across more sand to the next island. But as I drew nearer I realized it was not going to be quite so simple as that. Running through the sand were channels of water, varying, I should say, between ten and twenty feet wide. How deep they were I could not tell. Anyhow, I saw at once that I would have to take off my shoes and wade at least part of the way.

Just then I saw two men begin to cross. I watched them for some minutes, taking note of the places where they waded through the channels. I noticed, too, that they were hurrying, but did not at the moment understand why. I just thought that perhaps they had some urgent business on the other side. But there was a stronger reason than that.

Taking off my shoes and socks and slinging them around my neck, I began to follow the men. Crossing the first channel was simple enough, for I remembered exactly where the

men had gone, and the water was only a few inches deep. But
when I reached the second channel I was not quite so sure of
my position. As I walked into it I found that it was much
deeper than I had expected. So I backed out of it and, pulling
my trousers up above my knees, made another attempt. But
again the water was too deep. However, I was not seriously
worried, and walked up and down the sand till I saw where I
could cross in safety.

When I reached the third channel, however, about the
middle of the crossing, I began to feel a little uneasy. It was
much larger, I noticed, than when I had first looked at it.
Even yet the terrible truth had not dawned upon me. Perhaps, if I had been older, I would have understood what a
dangerous thing I was attempting, but I didn't know, and
there was no one to tell me.

By this time I had quite forgotten the place where the
men had crossed, and had to rely upon making attempts here
and there to find shallow water. But this time I could not find
it.

Then it dawned upon me that the water was no longer
still, as it had been. It was moving, and quite rapidly, too.
Bits of seaweed, pieces of wood, and sea foam were floating
by. The tide was coming in!

I turned seaward, and never shall I forget the sight that
met my gaze. Instead of a wide stretch of sand was a vast
waste of water. Indeed, it seemed—and the impression will
never fade from my mind—that the whole great Atlantic was
rolling in upon me.

The island of sand upon which I stood was rapidly becoming smaller and smaller. Every moment the channel beside me was getting deeper and deeper. Within a few minutes the place where I stood would be many feet below the surface of the water. I knew I must act immediately, or be swept away by the fierce onrushing tide. There was no time to lose.

Painting by Harry Baerg

But what could I do? If I did not know the way when the channel was shallow, how could I find it now when it had become twice as deep and was spreading out over the sand in every direction?

Yet somehow, even in that most desperate plight, I felt sure God would see me through. This was no time for long prayers. Every moment was precious. But I remember asking Him to guide me as, taking my courage in both hands, I plunged into the channel.

There was no use trying to save my trousers now. The water came above my knees, above my waist, higher and higher. Would my feet never cease going downward? For a moment I wondered if I had made a mistake, whether I should not return and try to find my way back through the channels I had crossed. But a glance behind me showed that such a course was now impossible. Everywhere the sand was covered. I could not possibly find the shallow places now.

Deeper and deeper—was this the end?

Ah! the ground was beginning to rise again. Yes, I must be halfway through! The water was becoming more shallow.

Yet there were other channels still to cross, all now submerged. How I found my way through them I cannot tell. I can see myself now, with the water above my waist, wandering hither and thither, searching with my feet for the shallow places, while all the time I could see the waters from the great Atlantic surging in around me.

Yet I did find my way, or I would not be writing this story now, and at last I crawled onto the island toward which I had set out so confidently less than an hour before. I leave you to imagine my appearance, with all my clothes dripping wet. What a sight I was! If there had been any children around, I am sure they would have laughed.

An old man came up to me and told me—just as if I didn't know it!—what a narrow escape I had had. He had been watching me all the time and never expected to see me get through alive. Very kindly he found someone who took me back in a boat, and I returned to my lodgings to dry my clothes and thank God for keeping me safe.

And now you will understand why I have marked that text in my Bible. It is found in the forty-third chapter of Isaiah, the second and third verses. I can't help feeling that it was written for me, for this is how it reads:

" 'When you pass through the waters I will be with you; and through the rivers, they shall not overwhelm you. . . . For I am the Lord your God, . . . your Savior' " (R.S.V.).

Little Shadow

WHEN YOU LOOK behind you on a bright, sunny day, what do you see? A shadow, of course. And when you try to run away from it, what happens? It runs as fast as you do, doesn't it? You can't get away from it, try as hard as you may. And why? Because it's yours. It belongs to you.

Well, it was like this with Ronald, only a little different. He had two shadows!

The first was the ordinary shadow that all boys and girls take along with them, and the other was—can you guess?— yes, his own Little Sister! There was no possible way of separating them. Wherever he went, she went. Whatever he did, she did. Whatever he said, she said. That's why Ronald called her his "little shadow."

Did she bother him? No, indeed. Ronald was glad to have a real, live shadow like this. A big, strong boy of nine, he thought there couldn't be anybody in the world so sweet and pretty and dear as his Little Sister; and she, only four years old, looked up to him as the most wonderful big brother any little girl could have.

77

◄ Color Photo by Don Satterlee

When Ronald started to water the garden Little Sister hurried and got her little can and watered the garden too. Whatever Ronald did, she did.

How they did follow each other about! You would think they were tied together with a piece of string, but they weren't. The thing that joined them was an invisible bond of love.

If Ronald began to climb a tree in the orchard Little Sister would follow him up just as far as she could go. If he picked an apple she picked an apple, and when he slid down the tree she slid down too.

Down by the gate was the stump of an old pepper tree, long since cut down. If Ronald sat on one root of it, then Little

Sister was sure to sit on the other.

If Ronald said, "I'm going to play in the sand pile," Little Sister would say, "So am I," and off they would go with their spades and buckets.

At play or at work they were always together. When Ronald went to sweep the front porch and steps, which was one of his daily jobs, Little Sister would take her brush along, too, and sweep as hard as he did. The only trouble in this case was that she didn't always sweep in the right direction, but Ronald didn't mind, for it was such fun to see her trying her best to help.

When Ronald watered the garden with his big watering can, along went Little Sister with her little watering can. They had a wonderful time together until their clothes and shoes were wetter than the plants, and Mother had to call them in to get dry.

When Ronald would sit down to read a book, a few moments later along would come Little Sister with another book and sit down beside him. Of course she couldn't read the book herself, but she liked to appear to be doing the same as he was. The funny thing was that if Ronald began to read out loud, Little Sister would "read" out loud too, only what she said was just any old chatter that came to her mind, and there was plenty of that.

It was Ronald's habit to say his prayers every morning; and just as surely as he knelt down beside a chair, Little Sister would dash to the same chair and kneel down beside him. When he prayed, she prayed, and the angels must have bent low to catch every precious word that she said, even though she didn't ask for the right things every time.

But it was at meals that Little Sister's efforts to copy her big brother were funniest of all. She watched every move he made and promptly did the same, good or bad, polite or impolite. If Ronald forgot his good manners for a moment and put too much food into his mouth, then sure enough the next

minute Little Sister's mouth would be bulging too. If Ronald, alas, began to eat with his knife, then Little Sister would quietly pick up a knife and begin eating that way also, until Mother caught them both at it and told them how very rude it was.

Sometimes Ronald would say, "I don't like carrots and turnips for dinner." At once there would come an echo from across the table, "I don't like carrots and turnips for dinner." In fact, just as surely as Ronald grumbled at his food, Little Sister would grumble too, not because she liked only the things Ronald liked, but just to do as he did. If he turned up his nose at rice pudding, then she turned up hers—that is, as far as it would go, which wasn't very far, seeing it was so small.

Then one day Ronald suddenly came to realize how great a responsibility was his. Coming in from school, where he had been playing with some rather rough boys, he accidentally used a very naughty word. Instantly he heard it again, repeated by Little Sister. Of course she hadn't the faintest idea what it meant, or whether it was good or bad, but coming out of her sweet, pretty lips it sounded simply terrible. Ronald was shocked. To think that he, who loved her so much, should have taught her to say such a naughty word!

He remembered then how she copied everything he said, how she was indeed his own "little shadow," and he made up his mind then and there that he must never say or do anything that would be a bad example to her. Just because she was willing to follow him anywhere, he must lead her in the right way. He began to see new meaning in some lovely words his daddy had taught him:

"I would be true, for there are those who trust me;
    I would be pure, for there are those who care;
  I would be strong, for there is much to suffer;
    I would be brave, for there is much to dare."

" 'There are those who trust me,' " Ronald repeated to himself. "That must mean Little Sister, for nobody could ever trust me as she does. I must be true and pure and strong and brave for her sake."

And he surely tried his very best to be that.

Clouds at a Picnic

THIS STORY CAME to me from a lovely girl called Geraldine who lives in a South American country.

One day Geraldine came home and found her mother, who taught in a church day school, greatly troubled because there never was enough money to do what was needed for the school. It needed new desks, new books, new paint on the walls, and lots of other things, but the school board said, "No money."

It was very discouraging, to say the least, and sometimes Mother felt like giving up her job.

"It's no use," she said to Geraldine. "I can't go on like this. It isn't fair to the children."

"Why don't we try to raise some money ourselves?" said Geraldine.

"Oh, we can't," said Mother. "That's been tried before and didn't work."

"Let *me* try," said Geraldine, who was in her early teens. "I'll plan a great big picnic with a sacred concert in the evening and invite lots of people. Then I'll sell food to them, and from the proceeds you'll have the money you need for the desks and books and paint."

"Thank you, dear," said Mother. "That's very thoughtful of you. But think of the work that would mean. You couldn't do it. And I'm too busy to take on anything more just now."

"Oh, I wouldn't try to do it all by myself," said Geraldine. "I'd get my friends to help me, and you wouldn't have to do a thing."

Geraldine was so sure she could do it and that God would help her make the picnic a success that Mother finally said she could do as she pleased.

So Geraldine told all her friends about her idea, and they thought it was good. They promised to bring food and help to sell it.

After this good beginning, Geraldine sent invitations to almost everybody in town, urging them to attend the concert and enjoy the food.

The day chosen for the picnic was the last Sunday in July. As it drew near, Geraldine became more and more busy trying to get everything ready. She didn't want anything to go wrong.

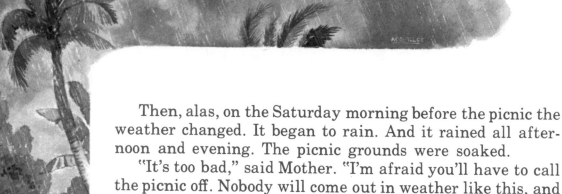

Then, alas, on the Saturday morning before the picnic the weather changed. It began to rain. And it rained all afternoon and evening. The picnic grounds were soaked.

"It's too bad," said Mother. "I'm afraid you'll have to call the picnic off. Nobody will come out in weather like this, and with the ground so wet."

"I'm not going to call it off," said Geraldine. "Everything's going to be all right. I know it is. God gave me the idea for this picnic and He won't let it fail. I'm sure He won't let it fail."

Sunday morning dawned bright and beautiful. The sun rose in a clear sky with all the promise of as perfect a day as one could wish for.

Geraldine was delighted.

"I told you so, Mother!" she cried. "I knew it would be all right. The people will come after all."

Then she lighted a fire outdoors and put a big pot on it in which she was going to cook the main part of the meal, the part she believed would bring the most money for the school project.

Her spirits rose. Then the most awful-looking black cloud came up and blotted out the sun.

"There's going to be a terrible storm," said Mother. "You had better bring that pot indoors now."

"No, Mother," said Geraldine. "I'm going to leave the pot right where it is! I have faith to believe that no rain is going to fall today. I know God answers prayer."

"But can't you see the cloud?" said Mother. "It's going to burst in a minute."

"I can see the cloud," said Geraldine, "but God is behind that cloud, and He's not going to let it rain."

In her letter to me, in which she tells what happened next, Geraldine says that she thought of *Bedtime Stories* and all the children who have asked Jesus for help in time of need. Then, while she watched the pot and the cloud, she prayed and prayed that it might not rain.

Geraldine went on with her final preparations, sure that God would not let the rain spoil the picnic.

And it didn't rain. Instead, that big black cloud gradually passed away and the sun finally came out again. But by that time it was too late.

That cloud had frightened everybody away. Nobody showed up for the picnic.

It was heartbreaking. Geraldine could hardly keep back the tears.

All that food, and nobody to eat it!

"You shouldn't have prepared so much," said Mother. "I

warned you that this might happen, with the weather like it is."

"It's going to be all right," said Geraldine, trying hard to keep back the tears. "I'm sure it's going to be all right. If God took the cloud away He can bring the people, can't He?"

But the afternoon wore slowly away. Only a few people drifted in. By six o'clock most of the food was still unsold.

Then came the sacred concert put on by Geraldine and her friends. They sang songs about Jesus and His love, and more and more people came, slipping quietly into the empty seats.

When it was all over, somebody said, "I'm hungry. Is there any food left?"

"Yes," said Geraldine. "There's plenty if you want it."
Everybody seemed to be hungry at the same time. They all made for the tables where the food was on display, and in no time at all, everything disappeared. There wasn't one thing left unsold.

So Mother got the money she needed for her school, and Geraldine learned something about prayer.

"Mother," she said, "I'm so glad I didn't lose faith when God didn't answer my prayer the way I wanted Him to. He answered it another way. I asked Him to bring the people to the picnic, but He knew we didn't need the picnic. He brought the people and the money to the concert."

How Terence Got His Train

FOR A VERY LONG time—it seemed years and years—Terence had wanted an electric train. Whenever he saw one in a store he would stare at it just as long as Mother would let him stand at the window. He thought that if only he could have an electric train all his very own, he would be the happiest boy in the world.

Over and over again he had come to Daddy and said, "Please, Daddy, do get me an electric train for my birthday"; or, "Please, Daddy, do get me an electric train for Christmas"; but every time Daddy had replied, "Sorry, Terence, but they are far too expensive. I just couldn't manage to buy you one; really I couldn't, much as I would like to."

Then Terence would go on hoping and hoping that someday, maybe, he would be able to buy one himself. The only trouble about that, however, was that Terence never seemed to have any money. If he was given a quarter or a dime he would spend it right away for some candy, or some little thing he had seen in the store, and so, of course, he had nothing saved up for anything so expensive as an electric train.

One day he came running home from school greatly excited.

"Daddy!" he cried. "Daddy! There's a boy at school who has an electric train, and he wants to sell it. May I buy it?"

"Surely you may, son," said Daddy, "if you have enough money." You see, Daddy knew all about Terence's weakness where money was concerned. In fact, he often said that Terence had "a hole in his pocket."

"I don't have any money," said Terence, crestfallen. "At least, I don't have any except that dime you gave me the other day. I haven't spent that yet."

"How much does the boy want for his train?" asked Daddy.

"Only twenty dollars," said Terence, "and he says that is very cheap because it includes all the coaches and rails and things."

"Twenty dollars!" exclaimed Daddy. "It may be cheap, but that's a lot of money these days. I'm afraid your one little dime won't go very far."

"I'm afraid it won't," said Terence.

"Do you know how many dimes there are in twenty dollars?" asked Daddy.

"No," said Terence, "I never added them up."

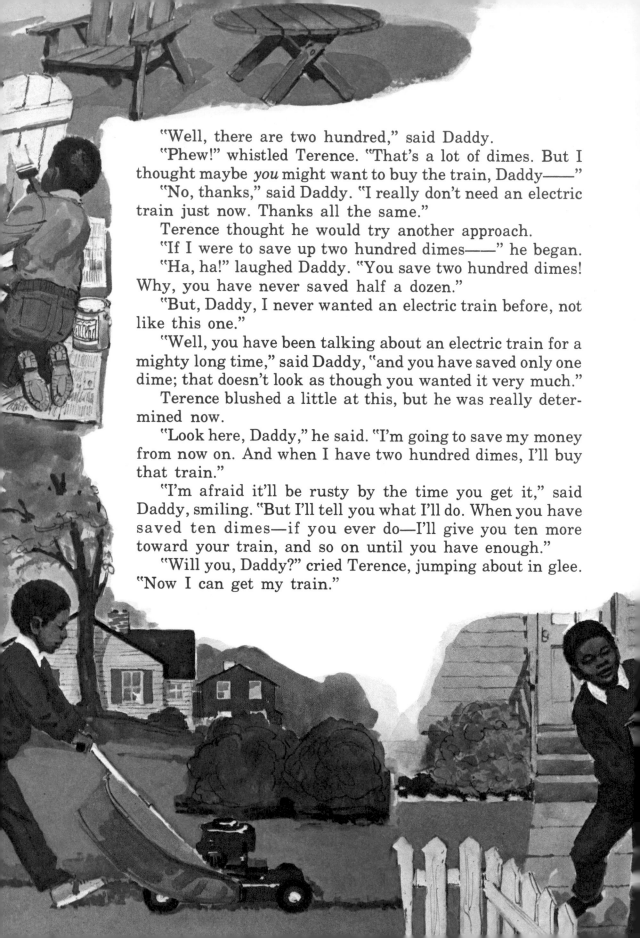

"Well, there are two hundred," said Daddy.

"Phew!" whistled Terence. "That's a lot of dimes. But I thought maybe *you* might want to buy the train, Daddy——"

"No, thanks," said Daddy. "I really don't need an electric train just now. Thanks all the same."

Terence thought he would try another approach.

"If I were to save up two hundred dimes——" he began.

"Ha, ha!" laughed Daddy. "You save two hundred dimes! Why, you have never saved half a dozen."

"But, Daddy, I never wanted an electric train before, not like this one."

"Well, you have been talking about an electric train for a mighty long time," said Daddy, "and you have saved only one dime; that doesn't look as though you wanted it very much."

Terence blushed a little at this, but he was really determined now.

"Look here, Daddy," he said. "I'm going to save my money from now on. And when I have two hundred dimes, I'll buy that train."

"I'm afraid it'll be rusty by the time you get it," said Daddy, smiling. "But I'll tell you what I'll do. When you have saved ten dimes—if you ever do—I'll give you ten more toward your train, and so on until you have enough."

"Will you, Daddy?" cried Terence, jumping about in glee. "Now I can get my train."

"I wouldn't be too sure about it," smiled Daddy, feeling that his contribution was pretty safe. "After all, you do have quite a long way to go. By the way, how do you propose to earn so much money?"

"I'm going over right now to ask Mrs. Brown to let me mow her lawn every week. Then I'll ask Mr. Morgan about sweeping up the leaves in his garden. Then I'll——"

"Now you're talking sense," said Daddy. "That's fine. Maybe I could find you a few jobs, too, if you want them."

"I do," said Terence. "Oh, Daddy, I can almost hear the train running round my bedroom now!"

So Terence started on his great new plan. Instead of wasting his spare minutes, he turned them into money, dime by dime. It was hard, of course, but then, every good thing costs something. When his friends would come to ask him to play ball or go swimming, he would say, "Sorry, but I have a job to do." It was hard—dreadfully hard—to see them go off without him, but just as he felt tempted to throw up his work and follow them, he would think of his electric train and stay by his job.

Yes, and he stopped spending his money on trifles, too, such as cheap toys that get broken in a few minutes. Instead he would take his precious dimes and put them in his bank. Of course, every time he had ten extra ones in it, he would call on Daddy for his ten.

Daddy began to get anxious. He seemed to be paying out

ten dimes every week or two. But somehow he didn't mind too much, for he could see that Terence was learning lessons of priceless value.

Months passed by, and the precious bank became heavier and heavier. Then one day—the very day before Terence's birthday—something tragic happened.

Terence came home from school brokenhearted. There were tears in his eyes and some on his cheeks and a lot more on the dirty handkerchief in his pocket.

"What's the matter?" asked Daddy.

"That boy's sold his train," said Terence, breaking down. "And now I can't have one after all."

"That's too bad," said Daddy. "Too bad. But I'll tell you, Terence, I was afraid of it all the time. You could hardly expect him to wait so long."

"I know, but I thought he would," said Terence. "Fancy selling it just when I was ready to buy it from him!"

"Well," said Daddy, "now you will be able to use your money for something else. There'll be lots of other things you'll want later on."

"I don't want anything else but my train," said Terence. "It's a shame. He's mean for selling it."

"Don't take it so hard," said Daddy. "Let's go for a walk together and try to forget all about it."

"A walk!" exclaimed Terence. "I don't want to go for a walk. And besides I'll never forget about it as long as I live!"

"Oh, just a little walk upstairs," said Daddy, smiling.

"Upstairs?" asked Terence, curious at once. "Why upstairs?"

"Oh, just for a little walk," said Daddy, leading the way.

Very much puzzled, Terence followed Daddy upstairs. As he entered his bedroom, his tear-stained face suddenly lighted up with surprise and joy. There it was on the floor— the very electric train he had wanted so long and worked so hard to buy.

"Why, it's my train!" he exclaimed. "How did it get here?"
Terence's face was beaming with joy.

"Oh, it just came," said Daddy.

"Go on!" said Terence. "It couldn't have just come by itself."

"I know," said Daddy. "I bought it from that boy weeks ago. When I saw the way you were working for it, I thought it would be too bad to have him get tired of waiting for your money and sell it to somebody else. So here it is. And you deserve it. I love to see a boy work hard and save hard as you have done."

"Hurrah!" yelled Terence, jumping right over his bed. "Oh, say, Daddy, if you'd like to come and play with this train any time, you may, you know."

"Thanks!" said Daddy. And the two sat down on the floor together and turned on the switch.

Steve the Steeplejack

STEVE HAD OFTEN seen his daddy climb up high and dangerous places, like church steeples and tall chimneys, to paint them or repair them. Someday, he told himself, he would be a steeplejack too.

It happened much sooner than he dreamed.

One day, as he was walking along, he saw a group of people standing outside the old Methodist church. At first he supposed they might be waiting for a wedding or a funeral, but then he noticed that they were all looking upward, and a few seemed to be pointing at something.

He hurried over and joined the group. Then he too began looking up. But he couldn't see anything. Only the quaint old shingled steeple, and there was nothing very special about that. He had seen it hundreds of times before and had watched his daddy climb it more than once.

"What's everybody looking at?" he asked the man standing beside him.

"Can't you see?" said the man, looking up and pointing.

"See what?" asked Steve.

94   "The bird."

"Bird?" said Steve. "What bird? I can't see any bird."

"Can't you see that bird tied to the top of the steeple?"

Steve laughed out loud. Whoever heard of a bird being tied to the top of a steeple? But he looked again and stopped laughing. The man was right. There *was* a bird up there. And it *was* tied to the top of the steeple.

"Why, it's a young pigeon," he said. "And it's got a piece of string around one of its legs."

"That's right," said the man. "And now will you please tell me how the other end of the string got hooked on the steeple."

"I don't know," said Steve. "I suppose it got caught on something as the bird flew past. What an unusual thing to happen!"

By this time more people had joined the group, which was getting so large that it was beginning to block traffic. Everybody was looking up, watching the poor pigeon trying to break free. It would fly a little way till the string got tight. Then it would fall against the side of the steeple. After much fluttering it would start off again, only to fall once more. "Poor little bird!" cried someone.

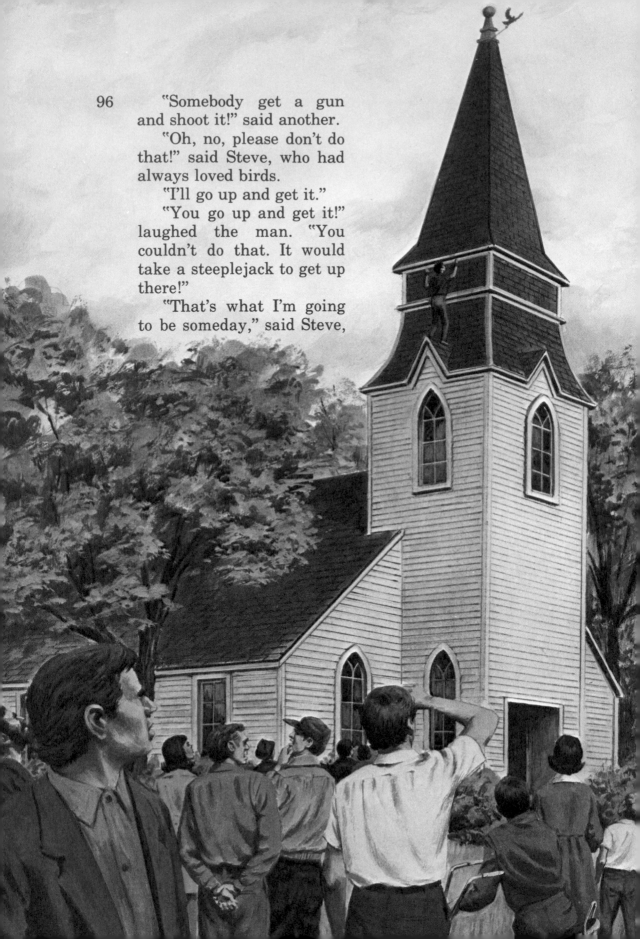

96   "Somebody get a gun and shoot it!" said another.

"Oh, no, please don't do that!" said Steve, who had always loved birds.

"I'll go up and get it."

"You go up and get it!" laughed the man. "You couldn't do that. It would take a steeplejack to get up there!"

"That's what I'm going to be someday," said Steve,

as he pushed his way through the crowd toward the door of
the church.

Fortunately the door was open. Slipping inside, he ran up
the stairs, then over to the ladder that led to the trap door
which opened onto the roof. Soon he was outside.

Suddenly there was a roar from the crowd below. The
boy had appeared on the church roof.

"Come down!" cried somebody with a big voice. "What are
you doing up there? Come down!"

But Steve did not come down. Instead, he made his way
carefully to the bottom of the steeple. Then, taking off his
shoes and socks, he began to climb. Flattened against the
steeple, he got a hold where nobody else would have found
one.

Now the eyes of all shifted from the captive pigeon to the
boy.

"Come down! Come down!" shouted half a dozen men at
once. "You'll fall. You'll break your neck! Come down!"

But Steve did not come down. He climbed steadily upward, inch by inch, inch by inch. How he held on, the crowd
did not know. But he did just as he had often seen his father
do, climbing on the stout nails that had been left here and
there to help the steeplejack. Keeping his eyes ever upward,
and never looking down for even a moment, he moved slowly
but surely toward the place where the string that held the pigeon was caught in a loose shingle.

Meanwhile the crowd had grown till it filled the highway.
Policemen had arrived to clear a path for the traffic, only to

look up horrified at the boy perched like a fly on the side of the steeple. One of them blew his whistle and ordered Steve to come down. But Steve didn't hear.

"He's going to fall! He's going to fall!" cried a woman.

"Come down! Come down!" cried one man after another. But still Steve went up, up, up. Little by little. Little by little.

Now he was nearly there. Carefully he reached up and grabbed the string.

Deep silence fell upon the crowd below. All held their breath. Now they were sure he would fall. Surely he couldn't possibly hold on with one hand and tug on the string with the other.

But he did. And to everybody's amazement he didn't let the string go as he might have done; he started to pull on it!

"Oh, no!" groaned the crowd. "Surely he isn't going to try to catch the bird!"

But that is exactly what he did. Slowly, and with great care, Steve kept pulling on the string, gradually bringing the bird closer and closer to him. Then he made a grab and the bird was in his hand.

The crowd gasped. How could he get down safely with one hand clutching the bird? Surely he was bound to fall.

Then what do you suppose Steve did? Somehow he stuffed that fluttering bird inside his shirt, buttoned it, and then, with both hands free, began to descend.

Down, down, down he came, while the crowd watched in fear and wonder.

At last Steve reached the bottom. Quickly slipping on his socks and shoes, he ran along the roof to the trap door.

Everyone shouted with relief when he was down safe and sound.

As the children crowded around him someone said, "Wasn't he brave to risk his life to save a bird!" (But that wasn't what his father said to him when he got home that night.)

◄ Painting by Herbert Rudeen

The crowd watched Steve in bare feet climb the steeple to where the pigeon was caught in a loose shingle.

100   When I was told this story, I could not help thinking of somebody else who risked His life for others. Somebody who climbed, not a steeple, but a cross; somebody who risked everything to save, not a bird, but boys and girls of every nation.

You know who I mean—Jesus, the friend of children. And why did He do it? That He might take you and me and everyone and put us close to His heart and keep us there forever.

The Mysterious Rider

ARE YOU LUCKY enough to have a great-grandma? If so, then, the first chance you get, ask her to tell you some of the things that happened to her when she was a little girl. I wouldn't be surprised if they prove to be the most interesting stories you have heard.

Grandma McAlpine was like that. Although she was ninety years of age, she could remember almost everything about her childhood; and how her grandchildren and great-grandchildren did love to listen to her!

One evening Frank and Bessie were visiting in her home, and soon they were trying to persuade her to tell them one of her grand old stories of the long ago.

"Please, Grandma!" urged Bessie. "Just one. We love to listen to your stories."

"Do, please!" chimed in Frank. "You know, Grandma, that one you promised to tell us about the mysterious rider."

A smile came over Grandma's face.

"All right then," said Grandma. "Make yourselves comfortable, and I'll tell you now."

Frank and Bessie sat themselves as close to Grandma as   101

they could and looked up expectantly into her face, knowing that a rare treat was in store for them.

"This all took place," Grandma began, "when I was a little girl of five, but I remember it as though it had happened yesterday.

"But to begin my story I must go back further still," continued Grandma. "A hundred years or so before that, my great-grandfather left the old country and set sail with his family for America. They settled in New England, and the children grew up and moved onto farms of their own. Into one of those families my father was born. When he was a young man he heard people talking about the wonderful West.

"Away out toward the sunset, it was said, there were thousands and thousands of square miles of marvelous forests, where grew the greatest trees that man had ever seen. The soil was so rich that it would grow finer wheat than any farmer had ever raised. In fact, there was everything there that the heart of man could desire.

"My father listened. It seemed promising to him. It was just what he wanted. So he talked to my mother, and finally they decided to go.

"It meant a journey of three thousand miles across open prairies, through forests and rivers and over mountain chains. And for a large part of the journey all their goods had to be crowded into one old covered wagon, drawn by two oxen.

"Tell us about the covered wagon," said Bessie.

"Well, just a word," said Grandma, "for we haven't gotten to the real story yet. Most of the covered wagons were built of strong thick planks. They were made watertight, so that they could be used as boats in crossing rivers.

"Usually several families traveled together, not only for

Painting by Kreigh Collins ▶

There were seven or eight other wagons in our caravan, and day by day we moved slowly on, just as fast as the oxen would take us.

company but to guard against Indians, who often attacked these caravans, trying to drive off the white people who were taking their lands."

"And did you travel in one of those covered wagons?" asked Bessie, her eyes wide open with wonder.

"Yes, I surely did," said Grandma. "I was only five when we started out, but I can still see everything that happened on that long, long journey."

"How long did it take?" asked Frank.

"More than six months," said Grandma. "We left home in April, as soon as the snow was gone, and it was October before we caught sight of Mount Hood, in Oregon, far to the

west. There were seven or eight other wagons in our wagon
train, and day by day we moved slowly on, just as fast as the
oxen would go.

"Some days it was very, very hot, and then we would all
get terribly thirsty. I think the oxen felt it more than we did,
because they had most of the work to do. I remember one day
we had traveled many miles without water. Suddenly the
oxen stopped. They refused to haul the wagon another yard.
Father took the yokes off them, and suddenly they started to
run. They had either seen or scented water more than a mile
away, but they were too weary to take the wagon with them."

"Did you catch them?" asked Frank.

"Oh, yes," said Grandma. "That was easy. They only
wanted to drink. Then we started off again."

"But the rider—the mysterious rider—when did he appear?" asked Bessie.

"Just you wait a minute," said Grandma. "We're coming
to that all in good time. Some other things were to happen
first. As we rode on day after day, week after week, month
after month, the poor oxen became more and more footsore
and weary. Father did not dare to let them rest very much,
for he knew that he had to get over the mountains before the
snow would fall. Then, too, the food began to give out. We
were allowed just so much a day, and no more, for Father
said that if we were delayed and ran out of food, we would die
on the way.

"And so, with the oxen becoming more and more tired,
and Father getting more and more worried, we moved on
westward. At long last we began to climb the Cascade Mountains. I can't think how anyone ever found a way across, for
there were no beautiful roads as there are nowadays, and it
was all so wild and rocky that we were nearly jolted out of
the wagon many a time. Still we went on, climbing up and
up, with the oxen panting and sweating in front, and Father
shoving his hardest behind.

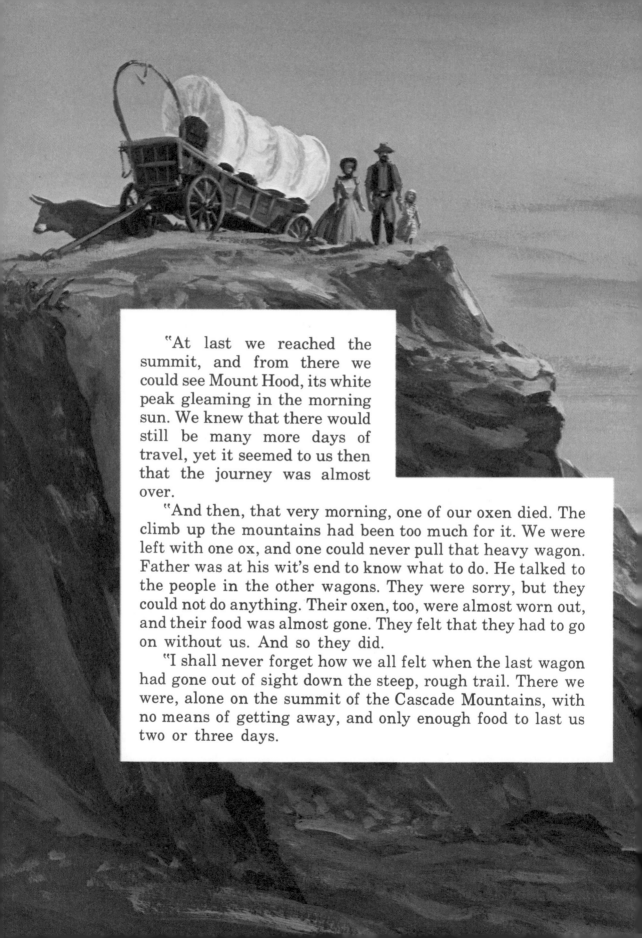

"At last we reached the summit, and from there we could see Mount Hood, its white peak gleaming in the morning sun. We knew that there would still be many more days of travel, yet it seemed to us then that the journey was almost over.

"And then, that very morning, one of our oxen died. The climb up the mountains had been too much for it. We were left with one ox, and one could never pull that heavy wagon. Father was at his wit's end to know what to do. He talked to the people in the other wagons. They were sorry, but they could not do anything. Their oxen, too, were almost worn out, and their food was almost gone. They felt that they had to go on without us. And so they did.

"I shall never forget how we all felt when the last wagon had gone out of sight down the steep, rough trail. There we were, alone on the summit of the Cascade Mountains, with no means of getting away, and only enough food to last us two or three days.

"Night came on. It was very cold. Father wondered whether the snow would come, and what we would do then. He kindled a fire and gave us something to eat, and then I was put to bed. But he and Mother sat up and talked about what they could do.

"By and by Father said to Mother, 'Surely the great God who has brought us in safety all this long way, through so many troubles, will not desert us now. Let us kneel here on the mountaintop and tell Him of our plight.' And there they knelt, the two of them, in the dark, with the cold wind blowing around them, as they told God all that had happened, and how they trusted Him to deliver them. Then they arose, and soon after that they tried to sleep.

"The night wore on. Upon our little, lonely camp the bright, cold stars looked down. Midnight passed, one o'clock, two o'clock, three o'clock. Dawn was just beginning to break when Father sat up. The silence had been broken by strange sounds.

"Clippety-clop, clippety-clop, clippety-clop.

"'Horses!' whispered Father.

"'Do you think it's Indians?' whispered Mother, leaping to his side. 'I'm sure there must be many of them around here.'

"'I don't know,' said Father, his voice very calm and steady. 'We must wait and see.'

"They stood quietly beside the wagon, listening and watching as the sound of the horses' hoofs came ever nearer and nearer.

"Suddenly out of the darkness came a voice.

" 'Hi there!' cried someone.

" 'Who is it?' called Father.

" 'A friend,' was the answer.

"In the dim morning light Father could just make out the form of a man on horseback, with another horse beside him. He walked over toward the stranger, wondering who he might be.

" 'Are you in trouble?' asked the mysterious rider.

" 'We are,' said Father, 'desperate trouble. One of our oxen has died, and we are stranded here with scarcely any food left.'

"Then the stranger told his story. 'At two o'clock this morning,' he said, 'I was suddenly awakened, and a voice seemed to say to me, "There is someone in trouble on the mountains; go and help him." So I got up at once, saddled my two horses, and started off. I was determined not to stop until I found the one who needed help. What can I do for you?'

"The mysterious rider took us to his own home and fed us. Then he lent us another ox, so that we were able to reach the end of our journey in safety."

"What was the name of the mysterious rider?" asked Frank.

"He never told us," said Grandma. "He just said we were to call him the Colonel, and we have called him that ever since."

"But who gave him the message that you were in trouble?" asked Bessie.

"Ah," said Grandma, "that is the most wonderful part of the story, for there was no telephone or telegraph anywhere near there. All Father could do was to tell God, and God did all the rest.

"All my life," she added, "I have never forgotten that terrible night on the mountains, when God sent the mysterious rider to our rescue. And, children, I want you ever to remember that the great God whom we love and serve never forgets His own. 'The God of Jacob is our refuge.' 'Blessed are all they that put their trust in him'" (Psalm 46:11; 2:12).

The Forgotten Packages

PREPARATIONS FOR CHRISTMAS were almost complete. Everybody was very busy, trying to get everything finished, so that Christmas Day could be the happiest day of the year.

The children were marshaled like soldiers, each having a number of things to do. And so, all pulling together, there was hope that they might get through in time.

Geoffrey's task was to deliver the packages of good things that Mother had planned to send to some of the neighbors.

"You won't forget any of them, will you?" she said to him. "These gifts may make all the difference between a sad and a happy Christmas for some of these people, so—*don't forget!*"

"Of course not," said Geoffrey. "I'll take them right away."

And off he went, his bicycle loaded with packages. Presently he was back again and off with some more.

All went well until Geoffrey met some of his school friends. They were having a fine time together and invited him to play with them.

As there were only two packages left at home to deliver,
Geoffrey thought it would be all right to stay. He could easily
deliver those two later on in the evening, he told himself.
After all, it *was* Christmas vacation and why shouldn't he
have a little fun? "Can't work all the time," he muttered.

So he stayed and, of course, forgot both the packages and
the time.

It was very late when he arrived home, so late that he
never even gave another thought to the packages, so concerned was he to get indoors without being noticed. Conscience, you see, was telling him he should have come back
earlier and offered to help the others finish the work.

It was not until after eleven o'clock that night that
Mother noticed the two packages under the kitchen table.

"Oh, that bad boy!" she cried. "So he did forget, after all!
I'll wake him up now and send him with them."

"Better not now," said Daddy. "It has started to freeze,

and the roads are very slippery."

"But the packages must go tonight," said Mother, determined that her plan should be carried through.

"Well, then, we had better take them ourselves," said Daddy, "if they *must* go tonight."

"All right, then, we will."

So, tired though they were with the rush of the day's preparations, the two started out.

"It will save time," said Daddy, "if you go to one address and I go to the other—only *do* be careful; the roads are covered with ice."

They parted, one going uphill, the other down.

Daddy was soon back home, but not Mother.

Where could she be? he wondered—and at that time of night too! Talking to the people, perhaps.

Half an hour passed. Daddy began to get very anxious. It was nearly midnight. He decided to go out and search.

He was about to open the door when there was a knock.

It was Mother, pale and worried, and holding her arm.

"I fell on the ice," she said, "and I've broken my wrist. Quick, call a doctor!"

What a disaster! On Christmas Eve too.

In the morning, when the children woke up, gloom settled on the household. All Christmas joy had vanished, for poor Mother was in bed in great pain, and how could anybody be happy now?

Geoffrey, though he said little, was the most concerned. Remorse filled his heart.

If only he hadn't forgotten those packages! If only he had done his duty first and played afterward! If only he had done what Mother said! How different everything would have been. To see Mother suffer so was the worst punishment he could have had.

Of course he told Mother he was sorry, that he wouldn't ever forget anything again, but somehow nothing could undo the past.

Christmas was spoiled. All the preparations seemed worthless. Everybody was wretched. Even the Christmas tree looked dark and gloomy, and the decorations quite out of place.

All because a little boy forgot!

One thing is certain, however—as long as he lives Geoffrey will not forget *that* Christmas, or the awful price of forgetfulness.

Why Leslie
Got Left

LESLIE WAS FOREVER forgetting something. When Mother sent him shopping, by the time he got to town he had forgotten what she wanted.

When Father asked him to wash the car he wouldn't think another thing about it until he saw Father driving out of the garage on his way to work. Then he would remember—fast— but too late.

He would forget to take his books to school, forget where he put his pen or pencil, forget the homework the teacher told the class to do.

It wasn't that he had a weak mind, or anything like that. His mind was as keen as any other boy's about baseball, swimming, skating, and other things that interested him. Certainly he never forgot mealtimes. He was only careless about those things he didn't really want to do.

One day the teacher told the class that he planned to take them on a special nature-study trip to a beach some miles away. Together they would explore wildlife in the pools and rocks by the seashore.

Everybody clapped. Such a trip sounded more like a holi-

day than a lesson. What a wonderful day it would be—especially as they were all to take their lunch.

"But there's one thing you must all remember," said the
teacher. "If you want to go on this trip you must bring a note
signed by one of your parents, giving permission for you to
go. Otherwise you will have to stay behind. This is most important. No exceptions can be made."

By next morning all the children had brought their notes.
All except Leslie. He had forgotten as usual. Not that he
didn't want to go on the trip. He wanted *that* very much. But
he just didn't want to go to the trouble of getting a note. He
thought it didn't really matter, anyway. So he forgot and left
it.

Then came the day for the wonderful trip to the ocean.
The eager and excited children, all clasping their lunches,
stood waiting to board the bus, which was about due.

The teacher walked down the line looking each one over
carefully. Then he spotted Leslie.

"Did you bring that note?" he asked.

Leslie turned red as a beet.

"I'm sorry," he said, "but I forgot it again."

"I'm sorry too," said the teacher. "But you will have to
stay behind."

"I'll run and get it now," said Leslie. "It's only a mile to
my place."

116 "There isn't time," said the teacher. "We have to go right away. Everybody on board!"

There was a mad rush for seats.

Then the driver started the bus, and away it went, leaving Leslie standing by the roadside.

He could hardly believe his eyes. They had gone without him! On such a wonderful trip, too! And all because he had forgotten a measly old note! A tear trickled down his face as he watched the bus disappear in the distance.

But hard though it was, the lesson was one he needed to learn. He was much less careless about remembering things after that.

19

Daddy's Birthday Present

DORIS WAS WORRIED. Daddy's birthday was only two weeks away, and she couldn't think of a single thing to give him.

It was the same old trouble. Daddy seemed to have everything. Handkerchiefs? Yes. Shaving cream? Yes. Tools? Yes. Ties? Well, Daddy didn't like to have anyone buy him ties. He always said a man had to choose his own ties. Socks? Well, maybe he needed some, but there was nothing very romantic about socks. Oh dear, what could a little girl buy for her daddy's birthday?

Doris decided to ask Mother.

"What can I get Daddy for his birthday?" she asked. "I can't think of anything he doesn't have, unless it's something he doesn't want or won't like."

"I don't know, either," said Mother, "unless maybe something for his car."

"But that would cost too much," said Doris.

"I know," said Mother. "That's the trouble. The little things he wants he buys for himself when he sees them, and the big things take too much money. I think the best thing   117

for you to do is to ask him yourself. Perhaps he will give you an idea."

"I don't like to do that," said Doris, "because then there wouldn't be any secret; and when there's no secret, what's the use of a birthday present at all?"

"I don't know what else to suggest," said Mother.

Doris thought it over and decided that she had better follow Mother's advice.

"Daddy," she said one evening, "I have something very important to ask you."

"What is it, dear?" asked Daddy, picking her up and setting her on his knee. "Is it a secret?"

"Yes, it's a big secret," she said, "and you're not supposed to know about it, but I'll have to ask you just the same."

"Go ahead," said Daddy. "What is it all about? I won't tell anybody."

"It's about your birthday," said Doris. "I've thought and thought and *thought* about what to give you for a present, and I can't think of anything. What *would* you like me to give you, Daddy?"

Daddy held her close to him.

"How sweet of you to be thinking about me so much," he said. "That's the nicest thing of all."

"I know," said Doris, "but I want to give you a present and I don't know what to buy. You won't let me buy you a tie, and I don't want to give you socks, and——"

"You darling!" said Daddy. "It's so good of you to want to buy me something."

"But what *do* you want?" begged Doris.

"Let me think now," said Daddy, wrinkling up his face. "Let me think."

Doris watched and waited hopefully.

"I know!" Daddy said with a twinkle in his eye. "I've just thought of something I want very much."

"Oh, goody!" cried Doris. "What is it?"

"Yes, it's a big secret," she said, "and you're not supposed to know about it, but I'll have to ask you just the same."

"It is something I have wanted for a very long time," said Daddy mysteriously, "something that I want more than anything else in the world."

"I'm so glad you've thought of something," said Doris, "but I hope it won't cost too much."

"No, I don't think it will," said Daddy. "I am sure you can afford it."

"Oh, do hurry up and tell me," said Doris.

"All right," said Daddy. "I'll tell you. What I want most of all for my birthday this year from my little girl is a promise."

"A promise," said Doris, suddenly looking very sober. "But a promise isn't a birthday present."

"But this one could be," said Daddy.

"But what sort of promise?" asked Doris.

"A promise that she will always tell the truth," said Daddy.

Doris' face was really long now. She remembered how she had told a lie the other day, and Daddy had found out. She remembered other times when she had told lies and wondered whether he had found out.

"That sort of present," said Daddy, "would be worth much more to me than all the socks and ties and handkerchiefs and candy in the whole wide world. It would be worth more than a brand-new Cadillac, even if you could afford to give me one."

Still Doris was silent.

"Would you like to give me a present like that?" asked Daddy. "I would prize it very much."

"I'll think about it," said Doris, slipping off his knee and hurrying away.

When Daddy's birthday arrived, on his plate at breakfast was an envelope marked "Very Private, Special Secret." Inside was a little note in Doris' handwriting. It read:

"DEAREST DADDY:

"I promise, with Jesus' help, always to tell the truth after this.

"With lots of love from
"Doris"

"That's my very best present," Daddy said, giving Doris a big kiss. "I shall keep it always." Then he put the letter in his pocket and went off to work, looking as happy as if someone had given him a million dollars.

They Gave
Their Best

IT WAS JUST A WEEK before Christmas, and everybody was thinking about Christmas presents. Edith and Eva were making lists of things they hoped they would find in their stockings. Mother watched them awhile. Then she said, "You know, dears, you have so many toys already, why don't you give some of them away to children who may not get many presents this year?"

Edith and Eva looked up in surprise. They hadn't thought about doing anything like that.

"Are there any children who won't get presents this Christmas?" asked Edith.

"Why, yes," said Mother. "Lots of them. And some live very near us. You know about poor Laura and Katie who lost their mother and daddy in the car accident. They must be feeling very sad and lonely."

"Of course!" said Edith, who always had a very tender heart. "They won't have anybody to give them presents this year—except the lady they are staying with. And I don't think she likes children very much."

"Let's look through our things," said Eva, "and see what

122

we can find that we might give to them."

Mother left them to talk it over. Soon they were turning out of their toy cupboard dolls, woolly animals, balls, building blocks, paints, crayons, and I don't know what else, piling them on the kitchen floor.

"Oh, dear, which shall we give?" sighed Eva, sitting down in the middle of all the toys.

"I don't know," said Edith. "But I suppose we should choose something extraspecial for poor Laura and Katie."

"Yes," said Eva, sitting down beside her. "I suppose we should. Do you know what I am going to give?"

"No, what?" asked Edith.

"Black Beauty," said Eva.

"Oh, no, not your precious cuddly toy dog!" said Edith.

"Yes, I am," said Eva, decidedly.

"Then I'll give Priscilla," said Edith. "Laura will love her. I'm sure she will."

"That's the doll you like most," said Eva.

"I know," said Edith, picking up Priscilla and giving her a big hug.

Just then Mother came back into the kitchen.

"Oh, my dears!" she exclaimed. "What a mess! I mean, what a lot of toys! Have you made up your minds which toys

124   you would like to give away?"

"Yes," said Edith. "Eva says she's going to give Black Beauty, and I'm going to give Priscilla."

"Oh, but, darlings, those are your very best toys!" said Mother.

"That's right," said Eva. "That's what we want to give."

"But if you give them away you can't get them back," said Mother.

"We know," said Edith.

"But Eva, you take Black Beauty to bed with you every night. Can you really spare him?"

"Uh-huh," grunted Eva.

"And Edith, you have always loved Priscilla so much. Are you sure you really want to give her away?"

"Uh-huh," grunted Edith, nodding her head.

"You are darlings!" cried Mother, sitting down on the floor between them and putting her arms around them both. "I think you are the sweetest girls in all the world."

Next day Edith gave Priscilla a bath and put on her very nicest dress. Then she helped Eva clean up Black Beauty and tie a new ribbon round his neck. After that they put the two lovely toys in a basket, covered them with a cloth, and waited impatiently for Christmas Eve.

At last the big day came. Mother said the two children could go to see Laura and Katie by themselves, which they were very pleased to do.

Holding the basket between them, they knocked on the door.

"Merry Christmas!" they said, smiling as the door opened and they stepped inside.

"Merry Christmas!" said Laura and Katie. "But what have you got in that basket?"

"Guess!" cried Edith.

"Guess!" cried Eva.

"We couldn't guess," said Laura and Katie together.

Then Edith and Eva set the basket on the floor and pulled off the cover.

"Oh!" cried Laura and Katie. "How lovely!"

"And this is for you," said Edith, holding up Priscilla to Laura.

"And this is for you," said Eva, handing Black Beauty to Katie.

"Oh, thank you, thank you!" cried the two little girls to-

gether as they danced and jumped about for joy.

"You'd never guess," said Laura presently, as she stroked Priscilla's lovely golden hair, "but this is the very thing I asked Jesus to send me for Christmas."

When Edith and Eva got home Mother was waiting for them.

"Why, I never saw you two so happy before!" she said.

"Oh, Mother!" they cried. "You should have seen how happy we made those two little girls!"

"That's the real Christmas spirit," said Mother. "By sharing happiness we make ourselves happier."

"But do you know what one of the girls said?" asked Edith.

"No," said Mother. "What did she say?"

"She said she had been asking Jesus to send her a doll for Christmas just like my Priscilla."

"How wonderful!" said Mother.

"How glad I am I gave my best!" said Edith.

"So am I," said Eva.

"And so am I," said Mother, giving them both a great big hug and kiss.

21

Swami and
the Crocodile

SWAMI WAS ONE of the brightest boys at the mission school, although, like some other boys I know, he was brighter at play than at work.

He had been attending the school for two or three years, but though many of the other boys had given their hearts to Jesus, Swami had not. He always wanted to "have a good time" and refused to give up some of the old bad habits he had brought with him.

Sometimes the people in charge of the mission had thought of sending Swami home, but again and again they had forgiven him and let him stay on. Someday, they hoped, something might happen that would lead Swami to love the Lord.

Despite all his naughty ways, the other boys liked him a great deal, chiefly, perhaps, because he was such a wonderful swimmer. In any sort of race he could leave them all behind, and this made him quite a hero.

One afternoon as they all stood on the bank of the big, wide river where they went to bathe, one of the boys dared Swami to swim across to the other side and back again.

128   No one had ever done it before. It was against the rules. Because of the current and the crocodiles the boys were supposed to stay in their own safe pool. But you know how boys are always looking for some new excitement.

And now, as Swami hesitated, they all began to tease him.

"You're afraid," one said.

"I'm not," said Swami.

"You couldn't swim that far," said another.

"I could," said Swami.

"Then why don't you do it?" said a third.

"Maybe I will," said Swami. "Maybe I will."

But as he did not go in at once, they taunted him some more.

"Let's see you do it!" they cried. "We'll count and see how long you take."

"All right," said Swami. "I'll try."

"Mind the crocodiles!" cried someone as Swami slipped into the water.

"Don't worry about the crocs," he replied. "I can swim faster than they can."

And he was off. With powerful strokes he worked up against the current. Then over toward the middle. While the others held their breath at the daring feat, Swami drew nearer and nearer to the opposite bank.

At last he stopped swimming and began to walk out of the water. At this all the boys clapped their hands and shouted, "Great, Swami! Great!"

For a while Swami sat on the bank getting his breath for the return trip. Then, as the others watched and shouted to him, he entered the water and began the long swim back.

Then it happened.

Swami had not been in the water more than two or three minutes when one of the boys saw a long, low shape moving toward him. It was like a floating tree trunk, but with hard, cruel eyes showing just above the water.

"Crocodile!" he cried, pointing excitedly at the large reptile.

Then they all saw it, and together they yelled, "Look out, Swami! There's a crocodile right behind you!"

Swami heard the warning and looking around, saw the terrible creature coming straight toward him.

He almost leaped out of the water. Never in his life had he swam so fast.

Always he had thought he could outswim a crocodile. But could he? Could he?

Terrified, the others watched the grim race.

For a little while it looked as though Swami might win. With a great burst of speed he pulled ahead. But no boy alive could keep up such a pace. Gradually the distance narrowed. The crocodile got nearer and nearer.

Suddenly there was a splash, a snap, and poor Swami disappeared.

With wild cries of fear and sorrow the boys rushed back to the mission.

When the mission director heard the story he ordered search parties out at once. Crocodiles, he explained, do not eat their prey as soon as they catch it. Often they bring it on land until they are ready for their meal. There was therefore just one chance in a hundred, he said, that Swami might still be alive.

So the search parties started out, combing every yard of both banks of the river, upstream and down.

Meanwhile, Swami, dragged under the water, lost consciousness. Then, in a narrow inlet, hidden by bushes, the crocodile covered him with mud and sticks and stones, fortunately leaving his head free and above the water.

◀ Painting by Harry Baerg

With a great burst of speed Swami pulled ahead, and it looked as though he might win, but the crocodile got nearer and nearer.

By and by Swami awoke to find himself in a crocodile's lair!

You can imagine how frightened he was. He was ready to scream with fear. But at that very moment he remembered something he had been taught in the mission school. He thought about Jesus.

"Jesus!" he cried. "Save me! Save me from the crocodile! And I will be Yours always!"

Even as he cried out he heard the tramp of feet. Soon he was looking up into the faces of a search party. Quickly they tore away the sticks and rocks, put Swami on a stretcher, and carried him back to the mission hospital.

Today if you were to visit this mission in the heart of Africa, you would meet Swami. He walks on crutches because of what the crocodile did to his leg. But he doesn't seem to mind. There's a joy on his face that is wonderful to behold. He is one of the finest Christians you could wish to meet anywhere.

STORY **22**

Digging for a Bicycle

WHOEVER HEARD OF such a thing! Digging for a bicycle, indeed! What next?

But it's true. He did dig for it.

"Then it must have been all rusty when he found it," you say.

Oh, no, it wasn't. It was just as bright and shiny as it could possibly be, all brand new and beautiful.

It happened this way.

Bobby, who was just 11 years old, had been wanting a bicycle for a very long time. In fact, he had asked his daddy for one over and over again. But every time he had asked, Daddy had said, "Sorry, Bobby, but there's no money to buy bicycles just now. I'm afraid you'll have to wait a bit longer."

So Bobby had waited and waited, and meanwhile all his friends got bicycles, some as Christmas presents and some as birthday presents. "Isn't there some way I could earn enough money to buy one?" he said.

"Now you're talking some good, sound sense," said Daddy. "That's the best way I know to get money for the things we think we need. Earn it! And if you do earn that bicycle,

133

Bobby, let me tell you that you will enjoy it ten times more 135
than if it were given you by a rich uncle."

"But what can I do to earn the money?" asked Bobby.

"Well," said Daddy, "I am very anxious to have the garden
dug, and because I do not have time to dig it myself, I'll have
to get someone to dig it for me. Now, if you would dig it as
deeply and thoroughly as anyone else, taking out the worst
of the weeds, then I would be glad to contract with you for the
job."

"And will you really pay me the same as you would pay
anyone else?" asked Bobby, a little doubtfully.

"I will," said Daddy. "You'll take longer than a man with
a rotary tiller, but the total amount I will pay for the job will
be just the same as I would give him. Now, Bobby, what
about it?"

"I'll begin right away," said Bobby, "if you'll show me
how."

And he did.

I wish you could have seen him digging. Such enthusiasm,
such persistence! Early in the morning, before he went to
school, Bobby was out at work, and back on the job again in
the afternoon when he came home. Yard after yard he
worked his way down the garden, with never a grumble or
complaint and with never any need for anyone to keep him at
it. He worked as though he loved it, as though he wanted to
dig the garden better than anyone had ever dug it before. In
fact, so smooth did he make the surface of the soil that it soon
began to look like a big brown table.

Daddy was delighted and said he would rather have
Bobby dig the garden than anybody else, at which Bobby
swelled up with pride and satisfaction and went on digging
harder and faster than ever. In fact, his mother sometimes
had a big job to get him to come in to supper.

More than once he stayed out till after darkness had
fallen, and everyone wondered how he could still see where to

◄ Painting by Harry Baerg

**Yard after yard Bobby worked his way down
the garden, with never a grumble or complaint.**

put his fork.

At last the long, hard task was finished, and what joy was in Bobby's heart when he came in one day and said, "It's all done, Dad!"

Then came the still happier moment when Dad paid up.

Bobby put the money in his pocket, feeling rich. There were other jobs. Then the day came when Bobby and Dad went to the city and began to look for a bicycle. And was Bobby careful about his money? I should say so! He examined every machine with the utmost care and asked the poor salesmen in the shops all sorts of puzzling questions. Finally he made his decision, paid over his money, and walked out of the shop with his precious bicycle.

Because Daddy wouldn't let him ride it through the 137 traffic, he had to push it most of the way home, but he didn't care, for it was sheer joy even to hold the saddle and the handle bars. And somehow, when he compared his bicycle with those of all the other boys in the neighborhood, he felt sure his was by far the best of all.

And if I may let you into a secret, Bobby still loves that bicycle, even though it is five years old, and he is much too big to ride it now. You see, digging for it made it worth so much more to him than if he had just received it as a present.

Maybe there's something you want ever so much and can't get because there's no money.

Why not try digging for it some way, too?

23

Alan and the Attic

ALAN KNEW PERFECTLY well that he was not allowed in the attic. Both Mother and Daddy had told him so over and over again. Yet he persisted in wanting to go there.

Why? I don't know. Perhaps because it was so gloomy and mysterious up there. Perhaps because some of his old toys were stored there. Perhaps for no other reason than that he had been told not to go there.

Some little boys are like that. Tell them not to do something, and they won't rest till they have done it.

Sometimes he would creep up the attic stairs, push open the trap door, and peep in. Then he would hear a familiar voice saying, "Alan, what are you doing up there?" and down he would come again.

"But why can't I go up into the attic?" he would ask.

"Because there's no floor up there," Mother would say. "I've told you that a hundred times. If you were to step off the rafters you might fall through the ceiling and hurt yourself badly."

"I wouldn't do that," Alan would say. "I could walk on the

rafters just as good as Daddy. I wouldn't fall and hurt myself."

"That's what you think," Mother would say. "All the same, just keep out of there."

Then one day as Mother was tidying up the front bedroom she thought she heard a strange noise above her. She stopped and listened.

Yes. Something or somebody was moving about in the attic. Could it be a rat? Or maybe a bird?

No. The rafters were creaking. Somebody must be walking on them. Who could it be?

It couldn't be Daddy, for he was away at work. Then who else? Surely not Alan! Not after all the times he had been told not to go up there!

"Is that you up there, Alan?" Mother called.

There was no answer. But the creaking stopped.

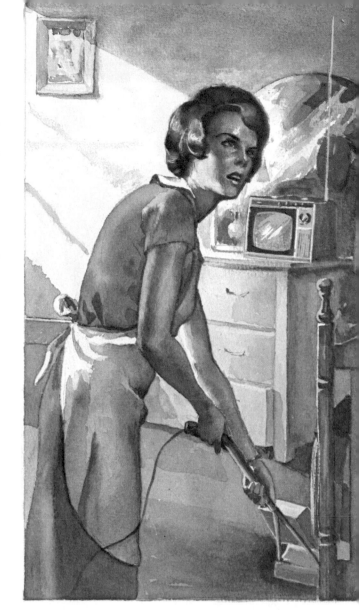

Mother stopped her dusting for a moment while she waited and listened.

By and by the creaking began again.

"Alan! Are you in the attic?" called Mother.

Again the creaking stopped. Now Mother was certain.

"Alan!" she cried. "Come on down at once!"

He came, but not the way she expected.

Suddenly there was a loud crack as part of the ceiling fell and hit Mother on the head. Then two feet appeared, followed by two legs and the rest of Alan.

Fortunately for him, he fell mostly on the bed; so, apart from getting splinters in his hands, he suffered only a bad fright.

Of course, when Daddy came home and saw the awful mess he had to clean up—well, Alan felt something worse than splinters. And this hurt wasn't in his hands!

Anyway, he told me himself that that was the last time he went into the attic and the last time he disobeyed his parents.

STORY **24**

Our World in Space

"HOW BIG IS THE WORLD, Mom?" asked Iris. She and her brother Norman sat by the fire for their usual bedtime story. On the TV, they had been watching men walking on the moon and had seen the blue-and-white earth in the black sky in the background.

"How big is the world?" repeated Mother. "It is very big. If you walked around the world you'd have to travel tens of thousands of miles, across mountains and deserts, rivers and oceans, and you'd walk for years."

"Boy! Would I be tired when we got back!" said Iris.

"I'm sure you would," said Mother. "That would be a trip twelve thousand times as long as our two miles to town."

"How long would it take to walk that far?" asked Norman.

Mother laughed. "I couldn't figure that in my head. Get a pencil and paper and I'll help you work it out. If you could average 10 miles a day, maybe twelve—let's see . . . walking around at the equator . . ."

After a few minutes they arrived at an answer.

"Almost seven years!" said Norman. "That's a big world."

"On TV it looked pretty small, from the moon," put in Iris. 141

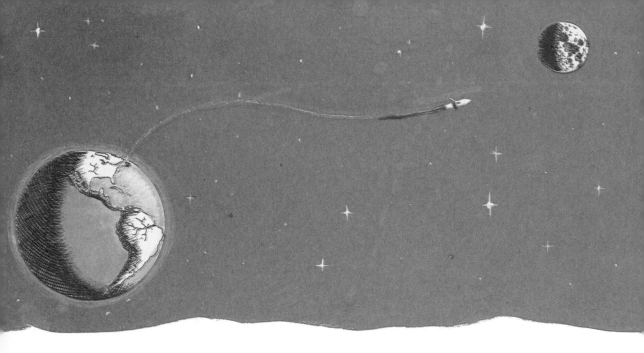

"Well," said Mother, "if you imagine the earth the size of Norman's baseball, the moon would be like a large marble traveling around it about once a month. Then picture this baseball, with its circling marble, going once in a year around a bright globe—maybe as big as our house—the sun. As the baseball moves it turns on its own axis. The people riding around on it—smaller than the specks of dust on Norman's baseball—have day on the lighted half, toward the sun, and night on the dark side, away from the sun.

"Of course you'd need billions and billions of baseballs made into one to make the world, and billions of specks of dust to make the people who live on it."

"Mom," asked Norman, "how long does it take the astronauts to get to the moon?"

"Well, first the spaceship is boosted into orbit around the earth. Then when it blasts off from orbit the moon is still a long way off—nearly 240,000 miles, ten times the distance round the world. The trip takes three days.

"When the astronauts start out, they travel at about 18,000 miles an hour to get into earth orbit, then faster than that to get away from the earth orbit toward the moon."

"Wow!" interrupted Iris. "That's fast! How can they carry enough fuel?"

"They don't use fuel all the way," said Norman. "Once they reach the right speed, they shut off the engine and coast. They fire the engine only when they want to change course. But they take enough food and oxygen for the round trip."

"What about a trip to the sun?" asked Iris. "Will astronauts ever go there?"

"They would be foolish to try," said Mother, "and they never will. You see, the sun is a great ball of fire, thousands of times bigger than our earth, and nobody would want to fly into that. A space capsule would be burned up long before it got anywhere near it."

"If it's that hot," said Norman, "why doesn't it burn us up?"

"Because it is 92 million miles away," said Mother,

"nearly four hundred times farther away than the moon. Even so, we think it nearly burns us up in the summer."

"What about the stars?" asked Iris. "Are they any nearer?"

"Oh, no," said Mother. "Much farther. The nearest star is nearly three hundred thousand times as far away as the sun."

"What a long, long way!" said Iris.

"Yes," agreed Mother. "It is too far for us to understand. We can't imagine such a distance. And the wonderful thing about it is that the stars, small as they look to us, are great big suns, just like ours. Many of them are even larger. They appear small only because they are such a long way off."

"How many stars are there?" asked Iris.

"Oh, I don't know," said Mother, "and nobody does. If you look up at the sky on a clear night you can see about three thousand, but if you look through an ordinary telescope you can see about a hundred times as many. And the more powerful the telescope, the more stars you can see. No one has ever yet seen them all."

146   "And are some of the stars really as bright and hot as our sun?" asked Norman.

"Yes," said Mother, "and for all we know they light other worlds like this and warm other people like ourselves."

"What a wonderful place we live in!" said Norman.

"Yes, and the more you learn about it," said Mother, "the more wonderful it seems. Our world and the moon and the sun and the stars are all moving, yet they move in perfect order. Every night we know just where to find each star, and we mark our days by the sun. You never hear of two stars bumping into each other, or of the moon going off into space."

"How was it all made?" asked Iris.

"Well," said Mother, "some people tell us nowadays that it all happened by chance, but I don't believe them. Someone must have planned it all and thought it all out first.

"We are told who did it, and how, in the very first verses of the Bible. Those are the verses that the first men to circle the moon, the astronauts of Apollo 8, read to the whole world on Christmas Eve while in moon orbit: 'In the beginning God created the heaven and the earth,' and so on."

Mother picked up her Bible.

"Let me show you what David says: 'By the word of the

Lord the heavens were made, and all their host by the breath of his mouth.' 'For he spoke, and it came to be' (Psalm 33:6, 9, R.S.V.).

"But now I will read you something else," Mother went on. The New Testament says that the one who really made this wonderful universe was Jesus. Listen to this: 'In him [Jesus] all things were created, in heaven and on earth, . . . all things were created through him and for him. He is before all things, and in him all things hold together' " (Colossians 1:16, 17, R.S.V.).

"Then Jesus must have been in heaven before He came here as a baby," said Iris.

"Why, yes, of course," said Mother. "You know that. When He was grown up He said that He had been with His Father ' "before the world was made" ' (John 17:5, R.S.V.). And because He made this world and knew it so well and loved its people so much, He left the rest of His glorious kingdom and came to live and die among men. It pained Him that one of His worlds had done wrong and loved Him no more. So He came to it that He might let His love for it be known, and that afterward He might make it all lovely as before.

"But there, it's time that you both were in bed. Let's say our prayers, and I'll tell you more tomorrow night."

25

The People in
Our World

AT THE NEXT STORY hour Norman and Iris
reminded Mother of her promise to tell them more of the
wonderful things they had been talking about.

"I wish you'd tell us where all the people in the world
came from," said Norman. "Johnny told me at school the
other day that men were once monkeys."

"That is a good question, Norman," said Mother.

"Did we all have tails once?" giggled Iris.

"No indeed," said Mother. "The idea that people came
from monkeys is wrong. I'll tell you the truth about it.

"The first chapter of Genesis, you remember, tells us
where the world came from—and the trees, the flowers, the
animals, and man. God 'spoke, and it was done' (Psalm 33:
9). I don't know how long He spent planning beforehand, but
when God was ready to act He merely had to say the word,
and the thing that He wanted came into existence."

"That reminds me," said Norman. "Johnny told me his
teacher said that people were something like worms at first
and took millions of years to 'evolve' into men."

148   "I don't think she said 'worms,'" said Mother, "but many

people believe that we came from lower forms of life. But 149
those people don't believe the Bible story of Creation. Listen:

"'So God created man in his own image, in the image of God he created him; male and female he created them' (Genesis 1:27, R.S.V.). Does that sound as if we grew up from 'something like worms' without Him?"

"I wouldn't like to be a worm," Iris interrupted. "It would be too easy to be cut in half."

"But listen again," said Mother. "'The Lord God formed man of dust from the ground, and breathed into his nostrils the breath of life; and man became a living being' (Genesis 2:7, R.S.V.). That is the true story of how men began.

150   "Again and again the Bible says that God created man. Nowhere does it suggest that man evolved through millions of years."

"But does it make any difference which we believe?" asked Norman thoughtfully.

"Of course it does," said Mother. "If man came from some wiggly creature in a swamp and gradually improved himself, there is no reason why he should love and worship God. But if, as I read to you last night, he was made by Jesus, in His image, then he will reverence his Maker, respect his own body, and care about his neighbor.

"Nowadays people are quite different from Adam and Eve and from one another. There are various sizes, and different colors of hair and eyes and skin. They are divided into groups that speak differing languages and think differently, and often war against one another. But they are all children of our first parents, who were originally made in the image of God."

"What does 'in the image of God' mean?" asked Norman.

"I think it means just what it says," said Mother. "An image is a likeness; God made man like Himself. And that is very wonderful when we think that God is the One who made the stars and the sun and the world and all that is in it. God made man with the power to think, to choose, to act, to love— to live as He lives, only in a smaller sphere. But man can choose to do wrong too."

"So people aren't like God now," said Norman.

"No," said Mother, "unless we let Him change our hearts and help us grow to be like Him. Now and then you will meet good people who love God and His Word, and who are 'true as steel,' and take pleasure in being kind. They may not look so beautiful as Adam must have looked when he came from his Maker's hands, but they are getting back some of the glory of God's image."

"What a pity it was lost!" said Norman.

"Yes," said Mother, "and Jesus must think so too. When He made man He must have hoped that he would always be beautiful. But we know someday Jesus will come, and then those who belong to Him will be like Him. The Bible says that 'when he shall appear, we shall be like him; for we shall see him as he is'" (1 John 3:2).

God's Plan for
Our World

"MOM," SAID NORMAN, as the three settled down once more by the fireside, "tell us some more about the creation of the world."

"All right, dear," said Mother. "I'll begin by asking a question. Why are there seven days in a week?"

"I've never really thought about it," said Norman. "I suppose it's because there have always been seven."

"Well, so there have," said Mother, "and for a special reason. How many months are there in a year?"

"Twelve," said Iris. "January, Feb——"

"That's right," said Mother, "but why?"

"Something to do with the moon," said Norman.

"Yes," said Mother, "months were originally marked off by the passing of the moon around the earth every 29 or 30 days; and the year, 365 days and a fraction, is measured by what?"

"I know," said Norman. "The earth going around the sun."

"Right," said Mother. "There is something in the sky that marks off the months and the years, but there is nothing in the sky that marks off the week. Yet there are always just seven days to a week. Each week begins on Sunday and ends on Saturday. I'll tell you how it began." Mother opened a Bible.

"The second chapter in the Bible says that at the end of the sixth day of Creation week 'the heavens and the earth were finished'; then 'God blessed the seventh day and hallowed it, because on it God rested from all his work which he had done in creation' (Genesis 2:1, 3, R.S.V.).

"Do you recall learning the fourth commandment? 'Remember the sabbath day, to keep it holy. Six days shalt thou labour, and do all thy work: But the seventh day is the sabbath of the Lord thy God: . . . For in six days the Lord made heaven and earth, the sea, and all that in them is, and rested the seventh day: wherefore the Lord blessed the sabbath day, and hallowed it' (Exodus 20:8-11).

"That is the only explanation that anyone can give of the week," said Mother. "It began when the world began, and

154 every seventh day that comes should remind us that the Bible story of Creation is true, and that man and this world, the sun, the moon, and the stars were made by the hand of God.

"And the one 'through whom also he created the world' (Hebrews 1:2, R.S.V.) was Jesus, as we said the other night. So Jesus was the Creator and Lord of the Sabbath, who 'rested the seventh day,' and 'blessed the sabbath day, and hallowed it.' "

"What is going to happen to the world when Jesus comes?" asked Norman.

"That is quite a different question, isn't it?" said Mother, "yet it fits in with all we have been talking about.

"In the beginning Jesus made the world very beautiful and placed on it two perfect human beings, created in His image. He loved them and was willing to do anything for them to make them happy. But they did something wrong, and because of it they lost all the good things they might have had. Do you know what happened later, after people became so wicked?" asked Mother.

"God had to send the Flood," said Iris, "and Noah and his family were saved in the ark."

The wonders of the world we know do not compare with the wonders of heaven.

"Yes," said Mother. "But as people increased again, they forgot God.

"Finally Jesus Himself came to the world and made very plain how much He loves us all. While He was here, He told His disciples something of what He planned to do for them.

"Listen to what He said: 'In my Father's house are many rooms; if it were not so, would I have told you that I go to pre-

pare a place for you? And when I go and prepare a place for 157
you, and I will come again and will take you to myself, that
where I am you may be also' " (John 14:2, 3, R.S.V.).

"Then," said Iris, "if Jesus comes back and takes the people that love Him to heaven, what will happen to the earth?"

"The Bible tells us that," said Mother. "Jesus will make
this world over again. It will be a completely new world, even
more beautiful than the old world was when it was first
created. All that is wrong and evil will be burned up, and in
its place will grow all the glorious things that Jesus planned
for this world in the long ago.

"The new world will have one big city, the golden city of
God, where those who love Jesus will live forever. They will
have lovely homes and gardens and fruit trees and flowers,
and nothing will ever happen to make them unhappy. No one
will ever want to cry there, for there will be no sickness or
pain, and nobody will ever die."

"I'd like to live there," said Iris.

"And you may," said Mother. "Everyone who loves Jesus
will share in all the happiness of that lovely home."

"So that is what is going to happen to the world," said
Norman.

"Yes, someday," said Mother. "That is just what the Bible
tells us, so it must be true."

"Do you think Jesus will come soon?" asked Iris.

"I think so," said Mother, "but, of course, no one can say
just when. He did say once that He would stay away until all
the world had heard the gospel; then He will come again."

"Imagine, Iris, what it will be to see Jesus!" said Norman.

"Yes," said Mother, "it seems too good to be true. But we
must let Jesus help us get ready for Him, so that we can have
a part in His kingdom when He comes." (See the story "New
Hearts for Old," in Volume I.)

◄ Painting by Harry Anderson © by Review and Herald

**In the beautiful home Jesus has been preparing
for the boys and girls who love Him there will
be only love, and peace, and happiness.**

27

Little Miss Grumbletone

OF COURSE THAT was not her real name. I couldn't tell you what her real name was, because she would feel terribly upset about it. "Little Miss Grumbletone" was the name given to this little girl by her daddy, and I suppose you have already guessed the reason why. Little Miss Grumbletone was just a bundle of grumbles. She should have lived in Grumble Town, but she didn't. She lived with her mother and daddy and brother in a nice, comfortable house. Really she had nothing whatever to grumble about, for she had a good home, good clothes, and plenty to eat. What more could a little girl want? Dolls? Yes, she had a host of them, and a beautiful doll buggy and a doll's bed. Candy? Yes, a little bagful once a week. Money? Yes, a purse half full of money that she was saving to buy a bicycle.

Then you say, Why did she grumble?

I don't know, but little girls are so strange sometimes, aren't they? They don't always do what you would expect

them to do. That was the way with little Miss Grumbletone.
She never seemed contented.

Grumble! Oh, dear! It began in the morning before she got out of bed. Usually it began with "Stop it, Jimmie!" Whereupon Mother would say, "What's the matter?"

And little Miss Grumbletone would reply in a grumbly tone, "Jimmie's singing, and I want to lie quiet in bed"; or, "Jimmie threw his pillow at me"; or, "Jimmie is making ugly faces at me."

At breakfast time it was quite the usual thing for little Miss Grumbletone to say, "I don't like this kind of cereal"; or, "If I can't have cornflakes, I won't have anything at all."

And then when she had to practice on the piano she would say, "I don't want to practice; my fingers are too cold"; or, "I've played this old piece over and over, and I don't want to play it anymore."

But dinnertime was worst of all. Almost every day, whatever Mother put on the table would be described as "horrid." When her plate was put in front of her, she would see something she didn't like and mumble under her breath, "Oh, this horrid stuff again!"

Now and then her daddy would tell her to leave the table and go out of the room for being so naughty, but this did not seem to do her much good. He said if she didn't stop grumbling he would have to punish her.

One day at dinnertime little Miss Grumbletone began to grumble again.

"Oh, I don't like this dinner a bit," she began; "you've given me such a lot of this horrid cabbage——"

"My dear," said Mother, "remember what Daddy told you before. There are thousands of little children who would be glad to have just such a good dinner as you have there. You must eat every bit of it before you go back to school this afternoon."

Little Miss Grumbletone, knowing that she must not disobey her daddy, pretended to eat her dinner, pecking away at it like a canary but eating very little.

When everyone else had finished eating, little Miss Grumbletone had still scarcely begun. Most of her dinner was still on her plate. Daddy left the table, and Mother went into the kitchen, while the little girl was left to finish her dinner all by herself.

Then from next door came the sound of the school bell. Little Miss Grumbletone heard it and knew what awaited her at school if she was late there. So very quietly she slipped away from the table, put on her coat, and ran out the back door off to school without saying good-by to anyone.

Then Mother came into the dining room and found Miss Grumbletone gone, and her dinner still on the table.

"All right, little miss," said Mother to herself, "just wait and see what happens!"

School over, little Miss Grumbletone came home as usual, having quite forgotten what she had done at dinnertime. All she knew now was that she felt very hungry.

Supper was ready, and a delicious supper it was. Little Miss Grumbletone thought surely someone special must be coming, for there were cake, jelly, and other nice things. She felt sure of a very pleasant time.

Then, just as they were all getting seated at the table, Mother walked in with little Miss Grumbletone's uneaten dinner.

"Little girls must learn," said Mother, with half a smile, "that they must not grumble at good food. My little girl must eat all this before she has any of the other things on the table."

How poor little Miss Grumbletone wished she had eaten her dinner at the proper time! Now it didn't look a bit appetizing, and, of course, it was all cold. The tears began to come.

"I d-d-d-d-don't want t-t-t-t-to eat it," she cried.

The others went on with their supper, and it was not very long before the good things began to disappear. Little Miss Grumbletone sat on her chair very silently, with her lips

162 pouted and a tear or two trickling down her cheeks.

Then the thought came to her that if she did not hurry, there would be no dessert left. She picked up her fork.

"She's eating it," said Jimmie.

"But it's not very nice of you to say so," said Daddy, who, with Mother, was pretending not to notice what was happening.

In five minutes all the dinner had disappeared, and smiles began to come out all over Miss Grumbletone's face. She was happy to get the last piece of cake.

When the children had gone to bed that night, Daddy said to Mother, "I don't think she will grumble about her dinner anymore." And she didn't.

28

Not on Purpose

PATSY, ONE OF THE NICEST girls in school, was sitting on a bench in the playground with her legs stretched out in front of her as she talked to one of her friends.

All of a sudden a group of girls ran by. One of them, tripping over Patsy's legs, fell heavily to the ground. When she got up she was very angry.

"You nasty, mean thing!" she said. "You tripped me on purpose!"

"I didn't, really I didn't, Monica," said Patsy. "It was an accident. I'm very sorry."

"It wasn't an accident," said Monica sharply. "I know you. You hate me, and that's why you did it."

"I don't hate you. Really I don't," said Patsy gently. "I wasn't even thinking about you."

"I'll get even with you, I will," said Monica. "You wait and see."

Seeing the crowd and wondering what all the hubbub was about, a teacher strolled up.

"Now what's the trouble?" she asked.   163

"Patsy tripped me up," said Monica angrily. "On purpose, too."

"Really, I didn't," said Patsy. "I just had my legs stuck out too far, I guess, and she fell over them. It was just an accident."

Teacher knew the two girls well.

"Monica," she said, "if Patsy says she didn't do it on purpose, you should accept it. She had no reason for tripping you up, and you shouldn't accuse her of doing so. Many times things that seem to have been done 'on purpose' are just pure accident."

Monica turned away, grumbling to herself about "getting even with her someday," and the crowd broke up. Soon everybody had forgotten all about the incident.

Two or three days later, however, they had reason to remember it, and this was how it happened.

The girls were playing baseball. Patsy was batting and hit the ball along the ground. Monica picked it up and threw

it in as hard as she could. But it was a bad throw, and the
ball hit Patsy a nasty crack on the head.

"Oh!" shouted Patsy, trying her best not to cry.

The players crowded round to see how badly she was hurt.

"That's Monica for you," said someone. "The mean thing,
trying to get even!"

"I wasn't!" shouted Monica. "I didn't mean to hit her."

"Yes, you did. You did it on purpose," retorted another.

"I didn't!" she said hotly. "It was an accident. The ball
didn't go straight."

Then Patsy showed her kind heart.

"It's all right, Monica," she said. "I'm sure it was an accident. I know you didn't mean to hurt me. And I'm sure you
wouldn't have done it on purpose."

Suddenly Monica remembered. It all came back to her. All

166 those unkind things she had said to Patsy just a day or two before.

"It's very kind of you to say so," she said. "And really, Patsy, it *was* an accident, I assure you."

"I'm sure it was," said Patsy, trying to smile as she rubbed the sore place on her head.

The other girls started to go back to their places in the game, feeling that something very fine had happened.

And it had. Patsy had shown a beautiful spirit of forgiveness, and Monica had learned that oftentimes things that seem to be done on purpose are really only accidents after all.

From that day on, the two girls were the best of friends.

29

On the TV

HAZEL AND AGNES loved to look at TV. In fact, they watched all the time they could.

Both of them, even little Agnes, had learned how to turn the knobs on the front of the cabinet, and they could "tune in" all the best channels just as well as Mother or Dad.

One or the other of them would start the TV going as soon as she got up in the morning, and keep it going until they went to bed. Daddy was out all day, and Mother did part-time work, so during the summer the children watched almost anything they pleased.

One afternoon as they sat together before the TV, there came the sound of angry voices, with guns firing.

"Good-ee!" exclaimed Hazel, clapping her hands. "It's the children's hour, and they're going to have another crime story. Let's call Mother to see it."

They both ran into the kitchen where Mother was busy preparing supper.

"Come and look!" they cried. "Please hurry, Mother. They're shooting already. It's going to be great. You must come!"

167

"I'm busy," said Mother. "I can't come now."

"Oh, do come. I know there'll be a murder," said Hazel. "Maybe lots of them."

"A what?" cried Mother, horrified.

"A murder," said Hazel, with a touch of mystery in her voice. "You know what that is, Mother. And there may be a whole heap of murders. Do hurry, Mother, please."

Mother decided to drop her work and go into the living room.

The TV was on, and there were cars racing and men shooting. The sound of guns firing filled the room.

Hazel and Agnes sat down again, their faces tense with excitement.

Then there came the shrieks and groans of wounded men, the crash of cars smashing into each other, and more shooting.

"They're dead now," whispered little Agnes. "Must be lots of people dead."

"Yes! Yes!" cried Hazel, hardly able to keep her seat. "I wonder how many were killed? I hope they got the bandits. Isn't it wonderful, Mother?"

"Stop it!" cried Mother. "Turn the TV off! Why, I never dreamed you were watching things like this. It's terrible, terrible!"

"Oh, but Mother, it's the children's hour," wailed Hazel,
as she obediently walked over to the TV to turn it off.

"Children's hour or no children's hour," said Mother, "I can't have my little girls seeing and hearing horrible things like this. No wonder you both have nightmares so often."

"But, Mother, listen, please leave it on a little longer."

"No. But you can try another channel."

Hazel turned the knob. Loud music came on.

"Oh, listen to that," said Hazel. "Don't you like it, Mother? That's rock music!"

"Hazel! I'm surprised at you!" exclaimed Mother. "Turn it off! Surely you don't listen to dreadful music like this. I never thought——"

"Oh, yes, it comes so often that we've learned to like it," said Hazel.

"Hazel," said Mother solemnly, "this has got to stop. I can't have my two little girls listening to things like this."

"Oh, Mother, can't we turn on the programs we like after this?"

"Not until you can distinguish between the evil and the good," said Mother. "And evidently you can't do that yet."

"Well, how can we tell what is good and what isn't?" asked Agnes.

"There is a way," replied Mother. "Long before there was any TV or radio, John Wesley's mother told her children that if they wanted to know whether a pleasure was good or bad, they were to take this rule: 'Whatever weakens your reason, impairs the tenderness of your conscience, obscures your sense of God, or takes away your relish for spiritual things;

whatever increases the authority of your body over your
mind, that thing is sin.'"

"I don't know what that means," said Hazel.

"Maybe it is rather deep for you, dear," said Mother, "but it means just this: We should never do anything, or say anything, or listen to anything that would displease Jesus or lessen our love for Him and the things that He loves. And I know He could not possibly want us to see and hear such dreadful things as we did this afternoon. We must learn to choose only the good things, and keep out the other. Our eyes and ears are two gates to our minds. We want to open the gates to the good things, the happy things, and shut the gates against the bad things."

After this Hazel and Agnes were much more careful. As they turned the dial, seeking for "the good things," they would ask themselves, "Would Jesus like us to see this?"

172　　　And soon they could tell, almost as well as Mother could, what programs to look at, and when to use the turn-off switch to shut the gates.

It takes brave boys and girls to shut gates, the gates of the mind—ear-gate, eye-gate, mouth-gate too. The story is told of the time, long ago, when Londonderry, a city in Northern Ireland, was under attack by a hostile army. While the city fathers debated whether to try to save the city or to leave the gates open and let in the enemy, a group of apprentices, boys still learning their trade, ran to the city walls and slammed the gates shut. The enemy was kept out, and the city was saved.

How helpful it will be, next time *you* are tempted to see or hear or say or do something you know is wrong, to remember to shut the gates!

How hard it is sometimes to shut the ear-gate! Yet it must be done. Whenever the enemy comes forth and tries to enter

Painting by Russell Harlan

You will strengthen your mind if you determine always to—See no evil, Speak no evil, and Hear no evil.

your fort by means of some impure story, some ugly language, or some evil suggestion, then remember the brave apprentice boys of Londonderry, and—shut the gates!

If the enemy should march along the road toward your eye-gate with bad pictures, on TV or in magazines, or in the form of some dirty book, then once more raise the cry of defiance and—shut the gates!

Again, if the enemy comes by mouth-gate and tries to enter that way—by tempting you to make a wrong use of your tongue—then again use your will power to shut off the evil words, the cross expressions. Shut the gates!

So you will defend the castle of your soul from all kinds of evil, and you will win the victory.

STORY **30**

Present for Grandma

LITTLE LUCY LIVED in a very poor part of a great city, just opposite a Christian mission. She was a good little girl and loved to attend the Bible classes.

One day, when Christmas was drawing near, the Bible class teacher talked about presents and how it is much more important to give than to receive them. She quoted the words of Jesus, "It is more blessed to give than to receive," and she hoped all the boys and girls in the class would remember to give at least some small token of love to their parents on Christmas Day.

Afterward Lucy thought a good deal about what had been said and wondered how she could afford to give anything to anybody. Her daddy gave her one quarter a week for pocket money, and that doesn't go very far these days. Somehow, she thought, she would try to buy something for Mother, and Daddy, and brother, and sister, but, oh, dear, there was Grandma, too! What could she do about Grandma?

Next time she went to Bible class she asked the teacher if she thought God would mind if she gave Grandma only a card this year. The teacher said she was sure God wouldn't

mind at all, and that Grandma would be happy to receive the
smallest thing if it was given in love.

So Lucy began searching for a card for Grandma that wouldn't cost too much.

One day she saw it. The very one! It had a picture of a pussycat on it, and Lucy remembered that Grandma had just lost her old tabby cat that she had loved so much. So she bought the card, paying one whole week's pocket money for it.

When Christmas Day came, Lucy took the card over to Grandma, and how pleased she was to get it! She said the picture of the cat was just like her own precious tabby.

This gave Lucy an idea.

"Someday," she said to herself, "I'll buy my granny a real cat. Then how happy she will be!"

A little while later she went to a pet shop and asked how much a real cat would cost.

"Four dollars," said the man.

Lucy's face fell. Four dollars! How in the world would she ever get four dollars? That would take all her pocket money for sixteen weeks—four whole months!

No, she couldn't do it.

Then she began to think that maybe God would help her. Now and then, when she was alone, and nobody could hear her, she whispered a little prayer, "Dear Jesus, please send me four dollars so I can buy my grandma a pussycat."

Her faith was great. As she walked along the street she would keep looking down, hoping to see four dollar bills on the pavement. But she never did.

A whole year rolled by. Christmas was drawing near, and still she didn't have the four dollars. It began to look as though she wouldn't be able to buy the cat for Grandma after all.

"Dear God, please help me," she whispered one day. "I do so want to make my granny happy."

Just then she felt something brushing her leg and, looking down, she saw a beautiful tabby cat.

For a moment she was tempted to pick it up and run home with it, but no, she told herself, "I'd love to keep it, but I mustn't. That would be stealing."

And was she glad she didn't! For just then a lady called out, "My cat seems to have taken a great fancy to you."

"Yes," said Lucy. "I love cats. And so does my grandma. I gave her a Christmas card last year with a cat on it. And this year I wanted to give her a real cat, but they cost four dollars at the pet shop, and God hasn't sent me the money yet."

"Well, well!" said the lady. "I'm surely glad you told me. You see, my cat is going to have kittens in a few days, and when they are old enough you may come to my house and choose one of them for your grandma."

"May I?" said Lucy, her face lighting up. "May I really? Oh, thank you, thank you so much!"

The day before Christmas, Lucy went around to the lady's house and there, sure enough, were four beautiful little balls of fluff. She chose the one that looked most like the cat Grandma had lost.

She could hardly wait until next morning to carry it to Grandma.

How surprised and pleased she was to get it! But she was happiest of all when she learned how it all happened.

"Isn't God wonderful?" said Lucy, as she finished telling her story.

"He surely is," said Grandma.

Frontiers of Peace

SOME YEARS AGO I was driving up the beautiful modern highway that follows the Pacific Coast from Mexico to Canada, when I suddenly came upon a very unusual archway.

At first it seemed to me to be entirely out of place, for it stands all by itself, with no fence on either side, and I could not help wondering why anyone should have ever thought of building such a beautiful archway in such an out-of-the-way spot.

But as I drew nearer I discovered the reason, for this arch stands on the invisible line that separates Canada from the United States, a border that stretches over three thousand five hundred miles, through forests, prairies, lakes, and mountains, from one coast to the other, without a single fortification or gun emplacement of any kind to protect it. It is truly a frontier of

Flexichrome by L. M. Quade, Adapted From Photo by Breidford ▶

The Peace Portal between the United States and Canada from the American side.

peace.

This beautiful and impressive archway is a symbol of the abiding friendship and good will that exist between the two countries.

On one side of it appear the words "Brethren Dwelling Together in Unity."

On the other side are words equally beautiful: "Children of a Common Mother."

Above, one on either side, fly the flags of the two nations, the Union Jack and the Stars and Stripes.

But somehow I was most impressed by the gates.

Gates! you say. Gates without fences!

Yes! The funniest little gates you ever saw, so small, so thin, and so weak that, if anyone should ever close them, the wind would blow them over!

But just above the gates, where they are suspended on the inside of the archway, appears this glorious expression of hope:

"May these gates never be closed."

Wouldn't it be a lovely thing if such archways could be built on the frontiers of all nations?

WILLIAM DOLWICK, ARTIST

Indeed, if such tokens of good will and friendliness could replace all the forts and fences, all the dugouts and trenches, all the "iron" curtains and the "bamboo" curtains, that stretch over so many thousands of miles of the earth's surface, what a happy place the world would be to live in! How many difficult problems would be suddenly solved!

Though this may be impossible with things as they are, it should not hinder us, as boys and girls, from building peace arches wherever we can and always trying to look at other children and their problems through them.

Although we cannot alter the frontiers of nations, we can at least see to it that there are no barriers of enmity between our hearts and other hearts anywhere in the world. In all our relations with other people—with the children at school, or the people next door, rich or poor, cultured or ignorant—let us remember that we are "children of a common mother." So far as lies in our power let us be "brethren dwelling together in unity." Let the gates of our hearts be open to all, with no national or racial boundaries to our sympathy and love.

32

Jesus Knows and Cares

THERE'S A BEAUTIFUL old hymn that tells us that Jesus knows and cares.

And He does care, especially for little children. You ask me why I am so sure? For one thing, because of all the letters I have received. They came in all sorts of handwriting from all sorts of children in all sorts of places, and they tell me how Jesus has loved and cared for them in special ways. Some of them told how they had prayed because they had read in some of the earlier *Bedtime Stories* about answers to children's prayers.

Each one has taken some little problem to the Lord and found Him to be "a very present help in trouble." Maybe you should do the same.

IN THE MAILBAG

The first letter I want to tell you about came to me from a little girl called Lily, who once went to stay with friends in a village named Pulloxhill, near Bedford, England. While there she loved to get letters from her mother, who lived in London.

Lily says, "One day I received a small parcel from my
mother and, on opening it, found a note to say that somewhere inside I would find a shilling [that was about fifteen
cents in American money]. Well, I searched and searched for
that shilling, but it was nowhere to be found."

Carefully Lily smoothed out every piece of paper, but no
shilling was there. She was very much upset about the loss,
for a shilling meant a great deal to her. It had been a long
time since she had had so much to spend, and when would
Mother be able to send her another shilling?

In her sorrow she turned to the Lord. "When I said my
prayers that night," she writes, "I asked God to help me find
it. I was sure He would."

And what do you suppose happened? Something very unusual. The next morning, when the mailman came with the
letters, he spoke to Lily and said, "Do you remember the parcel I brought you yesterday?"

"Yes," said Lily, "I do. It was from my mother in London."

"Was it all right?" asked the mailman.

"Why, no," said Lily. "Mother said she was enclosing a
shilling, but it wasn't there."

"Well, here it is," said the mailman. "When I got home

from my round yesterday, I found a shilling at the bottom of my bag. I have been trying to think how it could have gotten there, and it just occurred to me that perhaps it might have fallen out of your parcel because the wrapper was loose at the corner."

Was Lily glad to get her shilling? I should say she was!

"So that proves," she writes, "that God does answer prayer."

It surely does, Lily, bless your dear heart!

WHY BUD CAME BACK

Here's a letter from a little girl named Erwina, who lives in Texas. She writes to tell me how she prayed for her brother, and that's a lovely thing for little girls to do, isn't it?

It seems that her brother Bud had decided to leave home. Mother and Erwina had begged him again and again not to go away, but he had made up his mind, and it seemed that nothing could change it. Bud's suitcase was packed, and in a few minutes a friend would be calling for him. Then the two boys would drive away, and who could tell when they would return?

Erwina made one last appeal to Bud not to go, but it was no use. He picked up his suitcase and went out on the porch to wait for his friend. Not knowing what else to do, Erwina ran to her bedroom, fell on her knees, and begged Jesus to help

change her brother's mind so that he wouldn't make this big mistake. Just then the front door opened again, and in walked Bud. Erwina ran to meet him.

"I'm not going," he said. Then he went out to talk to his friend, who had just arrived. Bud told him that he had decided to stay with his mother and Erwina. The car drove away, and Bud came back into the house and unpacked his suitcase.

"He never knew," writes Erwina, "why he changed his mind, but I did."

Erwina is a sister really worth having, don't you think?

Here's a story that was sent to me from a little girl named Kathryn, who lived in Nebraska, where it all happened. It's an exciting one, and it all occurred when she was not quite six years old.

A fire had started out on the prairie and was sweeping toward the village where Kathryn lived. Everybody was out fighting the fire, except Kathryn and her mother, who was not well enough to go. But all efforts were in vain. The fire swept on, burning houses, farms, barns, granaries—everything in its path. Now it was coming straight toward Kathryn's home. Burning shingles were flying all about in the

high wind, threatening to set the roof alight at any moment.

"Let's tell Jesus," cried Kathryn to her mother, dropping on her knees and pleading with the Lord to save them from the fire.

After a simple prayer, she turned to her mother and said, with her face all aglow, "Now it won't burn our home. I know it won't. Jesus won't let it."

Just at that very moment the wind changed, and the onrushing wall of fire was swept aside as by an unseen hand. Kathryn's home was left completely unharmed.

Wonderful faith of a little child!

Marian and Norma, who live in Berkeley, California, were in a great hurry to go to school. It was almost time to leave when Marian noticed that one of their schoolbooks was missing.

"Where is the English reader?" she asked.

"Don't you have it?" replied Norma. "We *must* take that with us. We have to read from it today."

"No, it isn't here," said Marian, looking through all her things once more. "Where can it be?"

"Oh, do hurry up!" said Norma. "We'll be late for school."

"But we must find that book. Why don't you help me look for it?"

They looked and looked all over the place, from the kitchen to the bedrooms, but it was nowhere to be seen.

The precious minutes ticked by. Soon it would not be possible for them to get to school on time, and how they both hated to be late!

"Norma," called Marian, "let's ask Jesus to help us. Maybe He will show us where it is right away."

"Let's ask Him," said Norma.

So they knelt down and said a very short prayer—there wasn't time for more. It was simply, "Please help us find our book!"

As they rose to their feet, Marian said, "I know! There's one place we didn't look. Maybe it fell off the table into the trash box! Quick, Norma, let's run and see."

They did, and there was the book at the very bottom of the box. Joyfully and thankfully they lifted it out and rushed off to school, arriving just in time, as the bell stopped ringing.

STORY 33

Honest Tommy

IF YOU WERE to find a wallet lying on the sidewalk some fine afternoon, what would you do?

First of all, I suppose, you would look to see whether there was any money inside, and how much. Naturally, there it was! Then what?

Did I hear someone say, "Keep the money and throw the wallet away"? I hope not. I know that some boys and girls might do that, but not those who are trying to please the Lord Jesus and follow His golden rule. Their first thought should be, I wonder who owns this wallet? How can I get it back to him? I must do unto others as I would want them to do unto me. So I must find the owner as quickly as I can.

If you have ever lost a wallet, or anything else that you prized very much, you will understand. How you did want it back, didn't you? For a while that lost article seemed the most important thing in the world—like the lost piece of silver and the lost sheep in the parables of Jesus. And if you didn't get it back, you have missed it ever since, haven't you?

189

190   Well, that's one of the reasons for trying to locate the owner of anything you find. It's just being kind and considerate, and doing as Jesus would do.

Another important reason is that until you have tried to locate the rightful owner, you are stealing to keep what you find. And stealing is wrong. God has said, "Thou shalt not steal"; and we should be careful never to break one of His commandments.

What about that wallet, and what to do with it? The best thing is to take it to the nearest police station. Why? Because that is usually the quickest way to return it to its owner. Probably he has already told the police of his loss and is hoping against hope that someone will be honest enough to hand it in.

Then, too, it is a protection for you in case any question should arise in the future. Somebcdy might have seen you pick it up, or heard about your "good luck," and make trouble; but if you have handed the wallet to the police you are absolutely clear before man and God.

And that brings me to the story of "Honest Tommy." He was living in St. Paul, Minnesota, at the time, and, walking downtown one afternoon, spied a wallet on the sidewalk.

Picking it up, he looked inside. Then his eyes almost popped out. The wallet was full of money. He had never seen so much in all his life. Ten-dollar bills, five-dollar bills, and one-dollar bills. Fifty-three dollars in all. My, oh my! What a great fortune it must have seemed to him!

What did Tommy do with it? First of all, like a wise boy, he told his mother of his find. Then the two of them went to the police station and handed in the wallet. The police were greatly pleased to meet an honest boy, and promised to let him know should anyone call in about it.

Meanwhile the man who had lost the wallet was searching high and low for it. He couldn't think where he had lost it, and he was sure nobody could have stolen it. Finally, one of his friends suggested telling the police. You can guess the result. The police said, Yes, a wallet had been brought in by a young lad who had found it on the street. If the man could properly identify it, he could have it.

Imagine the man's surprise and delight when he discovered all his money was still there. Not a dollar was missing! So pleased was he about it that he asked to see Tommy,

and promptly gave him a $25 bond. He thought honesty should be rewarded.

Then somehow the newspapers heard about it. "Honest Tommy" found his name in the headlines, along with those of statesmen and big-league baseball players. A news photographer went to Tommy's home, took a picture of him, and put it on the front page of the St. Paul *Dispatch.* Thus the whole city heard of his honest deed, and was proud of him. Thousands read the story, and rejoiced that there was such a boy growing up in St. Paul, with a mother teaching him to obey the commandments of God.

The original picture of Tommy with the wallet, which appears with this story (taken by the *Dispatch* photographer), now hangs in Tommy's home, a constant reminder to him, his brother, and his sisters, that honesty is a noble virtue, and its lessons and rewards should be learned early in life.

And now, in thousands of other homes, through the ministry of *Bedtime Stories,* it will bring the same beautiful message. Surely Tommy never dreamed of all the good he would do and the example he was setting when, on that far-off afternoon in St. Paul, he did what he knew to be right.